7 Kingdom Keys

& their operational principles

Dr. Janet Bolaji Adegbenro

7 Kingdom Keys and their operational principles
Janet Bolaji Adegbenro

Copyright © 2019 Janet Adegbenro

ISBN: 978-1-928499-76-3
First published: July 2019
Print on demand

Published in South Africa

For further information or permission, contact:
Janet Bolaji Adegbenro
PO Box 996, Garsfontein, Pretoria, South Africa
+27 84 626 7389
Psalm138vs4@gmail.com
www.globalthronesministries.com

All scripture quotations are from the New King James Version of the Bible except otherwise stated

Editing: Alida Pretorious
Cover design: Duyile Opemiposi
Proofreading: Cecilia Klenyhans

Printing and binding by:
Groep 7 Drukkers en Uitgewers (Pty) Ltd
www.groep7.co.za

TABLE OF CONTENTS

DEDICATION

This book is dedicated to the Ancient of Days, the Lion of the Tribe of Judah. He won the war by conquering the grave, restoring the keys of the Kingdom and delivering them into the hands of His disciples so we might have dominion forever.

"But the saints of the most High shall take the kingdom, and possess the kingdom forever, even for ever and ever." – Daniel 7:18 (KJV)

ACKNOWLEDGEMENTS

My heartfelt gratitude belongs first, foremost and always to God Almighty, my faithful Heavenly Father, who gave me counsel in due season and instructed me to write this book.

Thank you to my beloved husband, Olugbenga Adegbenro, for his constant motivation to bring out the best in me and my precious children Goodness, Mercy and Peace Adegbenro for their support, understanding and prayers.

I am grateful to all the men and women of God who laboured in prayers until this book was published. May the Lord give you all an eternal great reward.

My profound gratitude also goes to my creative graphic designer Duyile Opemiposi. You are such a blessed son indeed!

I am most grateful to all the trained Throne Intercessors from the 2013 to 2019 set who have committed to training and practice of the operational principles in this book.

I greatly appreciate my Spirit-filled editor Alida Pretorious and my proofreader Cecilia Klenyhans. May you all be eternally rewarded by the Heaven of Heavens.

Finally, I greatly appreciate Pastor Yemi Ajimatanrareje and Pastor Wale Ajimatanrareje for opening up their churches at Open Heavens Church, Brentwood, Carlifornia and Royal Seed Church International, Maryland USA where l first preached the Kingdom keys and the operational principles.

ABOUT THE BOOK

The seven Kingdom keys and their operational principles is a prophetic revelation from the womb of the Holy Spirit to open the door to the supernatural manifestation of God's glory, authority and power so that you might dominate your Kingdom inheritance on Earth.

After diligently reading the seven Kingdom keys and their operational principles, you will discover the following:

- The mystery of the seven kingdom keys to unlock your Kingdom destiny and shine forth your glory;

- The hidden ancient secrets about the believers' Kingdom authority;

- How to open closed doors to your Kingdom inheritance;

- How to become a new, polished arrow in God's quiver;

- How Jesus used the Keys of the Kingdom and prevailed;

- The strategic use of the seven Kingdom keys to rule, reign and subdue the kingdom of darkness and dominate your inheritance on Earth; and

- The secret to winning every battle in life and fulfilling your Kingdom mandate.

Note

Most of the quotes from the Bible come from the New International Version and are marked as such. If a quote is unmarked, it comes from my beloved New King James Version and they have been left that way by my editor for the sheer beauty of the Word.

PREFACE

VISION OF THE DISPENSATIONAL ANGELS OF RESTORATION

"And I tell you that you are Peter, and on this rock I will build my church, and the gates of Hades will not overcome it." – Matthew 16:18 (NIV)

The entire world is in confusion due to the war that the kingdom of darkness is waging against the Church, stealing and destroying the Kingdom inheritance of believers. The battle is constantly becoming fiercer in fulfillment of the end-time prophecies.

I felt greatly burdened by the confusion, calamities, terrorism, iniquities and end-time viruses plaguing the world and crippling even the super power nations. I started asking God to give me a clear understanding of the keys to the Kingdom that the Lord Jesus has promised to give unto the body of Christ, as well as the operational principles on how to apply these keys.

"I will give you the keys of the kingdom of heaven; whatever you bind on earth will be bound in heaven, and whatever you loose on earth will be loosed in heaven." – Matthew 16:19 (NIV)

The ever-merciful Father answered my prayers by giving me seven powerful Kingdom keys with practical demonstrations of the operational principles and strategic spiritual warfare prayers to reign, rule, subdue and dominate our Kingdom inheritance during the end times.

After I received the revelation of the seven keys, I started asking God specific questions, as we were crossing over into 2017.

I asked God:

- "Lord, what is burning in Your heart, that You want me to do in the new year? I only want to be involved in and busy with whatever is burning in your heart."

- "What must I do specifically with these keys of the Kingdom that will be pleasing to your heart?"

God answered my prayers with a vision. I saw soldiers with swords driving in an open-roofed car. A tall man stood upright in the car. He was covered in fresh blood from head to toe. The car moved like a hurricane and it hovered above the ground. I shivered with the power from this vision.

I then asked the Lord who these people were and what their mission on Earth was. The Lord replied that His heart burned for a season of restoring His glory. He said that His glory had departed from the earth and everything on it – the youth, His people, kings, queens, the Church, families, marriages and nations. The soldiers in my vision were dispensational Angels of restoration whom He had sent to restore His glory from a mobile throne with the blood of His everlasting covenant at the centre of the throne.

"Cooperate with these Angels of restoration to restore My glory before My return, using the seven keys of the Kingdom that I have delivered into your hands and the authority that I have delegated to you, God told me.

"For the earth will be filled with the knowledge of the glory of the Lord as the waters cover the sea." – Habakkuk 2:14 (NIV)

It is imperative to be involved in the restoration of God's glory among the nations on Earth. The restoration of His glory is paramount in God's heart before the second coming of the Lord Jesus. So how do we restore His glory and order on Earth? How do we change our environment and atmosphere to establish the Kingdom of God? How do we manifest the glory of God and dominate the earth?

Jesus Christ gave the promise of the Kingdom keys to the disciples after He ensured that they had a revelation of who He really is and knew His divine personality as Christ Jesus, the Son of the living God.

Jesus revealed deep mysteries to the disciples about His redemptive purpose on Earth, including what he would have to suffer and how He would accomplish His mission of redemption. His goal was to retrieve the keys to the Kingdom that Satan has stolen from Adam and return them to His saints with His delegated authority. We must use the keys to subdue the kingdom of darkness, reign over it in God's authority and have dominion over the earth to the glory of God's Name.

Jesus waited for His disciples to understand His divine identity and His redemptive purpose before he unfolded the mystery of His suffering, shameful death and resurrection as a means to retrieve the keys of the Kingdom to them.

The time to awaken God's glory in your life is now. It is the season to shine forth the glory of God with a clear understanding of the Kingdom keys. Learn how to use these keys effectively to subdue principalities and the power of darkness in the first and second Heaven and dominate the earth.

To the glory of God the Father, ninety percent of the revelations in this book were downloaded from the Throne of Grace unto me for each chapter as I interceded continually in the process of writing the book.

As you read this book, you will no longer be oppressed and imprisoned in fear by the accuser of the brethren. Every yoke that has held you down with spiritual mediocrity and hindered your growth into maturity will be broken and the full knowledge of your inheritance in Christ Jesus will be unlocked.

There will be a great spiritual awakening and new fire in your bones that will bring complete transformation with deep revelation of the Kingdom of God to manifest His glory and power on Earth. God gave me these revelations with clear instructions to write this book as a blessing to this generation and generations to come.

Let this book fill you with courage and clear knowledge of your Kingdom destiny and the inheritance of the saints in Christ Jesus, with the understanding of the power that works within you to do the works of God's good pleasure.

My earnest and fervent prayers as you read the book, is that the eyes of your understanding will be enlightened and your bones will be ignited with fire that will surely bring a powerful paradigm shift by the power of the Holy Spirit to manifest the glory of God on this planet and fulfill your eternal Kingdom mandate.

Dr Janet Bolaji Adegbenro
Pretoria, South Africa
June   **2019**

CHAPTER 1

MYSTERY OF THE KINGDOM

"For the kingdom of God is not a matter of eating and drinking, but of righteousness, peace and joy in the Holy Spirit, because anyone who serves Christ in this way is pleasing to God and receives human approval." – Romans 14:1718 (NIV)

"The Lord has established His Throne in heaven, and His Kingdom rules over all" – Psalm 103:19 (NIV)

The Kingdom of God is His sovereign government on Earth. The Greek word for "Kingdom" is basileia, which means "royal power" and "sovereignty". It originates from the root word basileus, which relates to the idea of a foundation of power.

The Creator placed the Kingdom concept in the heart of man from inception. A kingdom is a state ruled and governed by a king. There is no kingdom without a king to rule and govern the kingdom and dominate the territory as an inheritance.

God's Kingdom concept was His original purpose for creating man. God's purpose for us on Earth is to understand His Kingdom and our authority in it. When we have a clear understanding of the Kingdom of God in its totality, we cooperate with God to work it out in alignment with His Kingdom purpose on Earth.

"Then God said, "Let us make mankind in our image, in our likeness, so that they may rule over the fish in the sea and the birds in the sky, over the livestock and all the wild animals,[a] and over all the creatures that move along the ground." So God created mankind in his own image, in the image of God he created them; male and female he created them. God blessed them and said to them, "Be fruitful and increase in number; fill the earth and subdue it. Rule over the fish in the sea and the birds in the sky and over every living creature that moves on the ground." – Genesis 1: 26 – 28 (NIV)

"Do not be afraid, little flock, for your Father has been pleased to give you the kingdom. – Luke 12:32 (NIV)

God is sovereign over His spiritual enemy, Satan, who seeks to dominate the earth with his darkness to counteract God's Kingdom of light. God governs over all that He has created, including human beings, territories, animals and nations. He is the Supreme Ruler of the planet. Satan has created nothing but only likes to imitate. God has created human beings in His own image and characteristics to manage the earth and all the resources and the fullness thereof to His pleasure and glory.

God's supreme invisible Spirit influences the visible, physical and natural world by means of men and women who are born by the Spirit into His eternal Kingdom. The Kingdom of God is the manifestation of the spiritual realm that demonstrates His Lordship, dominion and sovereign will.

The church of God and the whole earth is supposed to be governed by the Kingdom principles, Kingdom lifestyle and Kingdom purposes according to God's will, rather than the will of an earthly doctrinal mindset. The revelation of the Kingdom concept, with the understanding of your Kingdom identity, who you are originally and your spiritual DNA in Christ Jesus as God's likeness and image, will change your orientation and mindset in life and enable you to attain greatness.

The Kingdom of God includes these components:

- A King;
- A domain;
- A constitution for governance;
- Principles;
- Subjects;
- Privileges and benefits;
- Procedures and order;
- An army; and
- Security.

"Once, on being asked by the Pharisees when the kingdom of God would come, Jesus replied, "The coming of the kingdom of God is not something that can be observed, nor will people say, 'Here it is,' or 'There it is,' because the kingdom of God is in your midst. – Luke 17:20 21 (NIV)

The clear understanding of the Kingdom of God within us changes our spiritual orientation, our vision and the way we pray and stir up our spirit to take hold of our inheritance. Presently, the concept of the purpose of God's Kingdom is alien to the Church. The Church does not affect the purpose of the Kingdom of God. The Church is mostly becoming irrelevant to the purpose of His Kingdom. It is no wonder that the kingdom of darkness is prevailing against the inheritance of the saints of God.

The understanding of the concept of the Kingdom of God by the saints will enhance the reawakening of the Church to take hold of their inheritance and dominate their possessions. Jesus taught the disciples the Lord's Prayer for a reason – it includes the focus and the content of the Kingdom.

"And when you pray, do not keep on babbling like pagans, for they think they will be heard because of their many words. Do not be like them, for your Father knows what you need before you ask him.
"This, then, is how you should pray:

"Our Father in heaven
hallowed be your name,
your kingdom come,
your will be done,
on earth as it is in heaven.
Give us today our daily bread.
And forgive us our debts,
as we also have forgiven our debtors.
And lead us not into temptation, but deliver us from the evil
one." – Matthew 6:7-13 (NIV)

Every human being born on this earth is responsible for activating his or her Kingdom identity and potential to fulfill the Kingdom purpose. We all have assignments to fulfill on earth. No one is born here on earth without a specific assignment to fulfill. This is the reason why God gave everyone gifts and potential with the measure of grace to activate and use their potential to affect creation positively. Surely, we will give account of how we use the gifts and talents that God endowed us with, God will judge us on how we developed and used these gifts.

"But to each one of us grace has been given as Christ apportioned it. – Ephesians 4:7.

KINGDOM VERSUS RELIGION

The reality of the Kingdom is the power of God dwelling in us as a life-long phenomenon. God's original purpose was

5

not to have a religion on Earth, but to have a Kingdom with delegated authority and power to manage creation.

Religious legalism is using your own ability and understanding instead of God's grace. Kingdom grace enables you to do supernatural things that surpass your natural human ability. Religion will make you struggle all your life to live a holy life to be pure, and wanting to please God with all your religious activities in your own strength. A religious spirit that brings a covering of darkness over the eyes and the heart and blocks your understanding of your Kingdom identity often controls religious activities and a religious mindset.

Religion follows the letter and the law but denies the power in the law and the Kingdom. Salvation makes you a new creature in Christ Jesus and understanding the Kingdom will establish the covenant of peace within you and give you righteousness and everlasting joy in the Holy Spirit.

We are saved by the Kingdom grace – not by our religious works and activities. Therefore, we must rely completely on the Kingdom grace, understand the depth of what the Kingdom of God means and receive the totality of the Kingdom, which was Jesus' message throughout His ministries and the gospel of the Kingdom.

The Kingdom makes you into the person whom God has originally created you to be. Religion limits you and makes you into a person whom God does not intend you to be. Religion is full of activities that does not align with God's heart. Religion does not bear good fruit and God only rewards good fruit – not activities.

Being a religious person with dedicated activities without the revelation of the Kingdom is a waste of your time and precious life. Remember, time is life!

Kingdom has to do with influence - the Kingdom influences the territory positively. You can only be productive, fruitful and multiply when you use your gifts and potential with your Kingdom authority to affect the world positively.

The governing power to rule the earth has been given to us through the death and resurrection of our Lord and savior Jesus Christ.

Jesus Christ came to preach the gospel of the Kingdom and establish the Kingdom of Heaven on Earth – not religion.

We have a trinity of sovereignties under whose authority we have dominion over the planet: the sovereign God the Father, the Son and the Holy Spirit.

CHAPTER 2

THE POWER OF REVELATION

"I keep asking that the God of our Lord Jesus Christ, the glorious Father, may give you the Spirit[a] of wisdom and revelation, so that you may know him better. – Ephesians 1:17.

Your victories, successes and fulfillment of Kingdom purpose in life depend on the revelation knowledge of the sovereignty of God, the will of His Kingdom, His resurrection and His word. The level of your understanding of God determines the level of your relationship with Him.

Revelation brings transformation. In order to anchor our spirit in Christ Jesus after genuine repentance and new birth into the Kingdom of God, we must have spiritual understanding of the word of God, because God's word is Spirit and it is life. Originally, God designed and created man to be a daily recipient of revelation knowledge of who He is and His Kingdom.

Adam and Eve received daily revelation from God during the cool part of the day. Jesus also received revelation from God the Father throughout His ministry on Earth. He did nothing of His own initiative, but only what He heard and saw the Father doing.

"Jesus gave them this answer: "Very truly I tell you, the Son can do nothing by himself; he can do only what he sees his Father doing, because whatever the Father does the Son also does." – John 5:19 (NIV).

WHAT IS REVELATION?

Revelation is clear knowledge and understanding of the vision of God. Revelation is an intuitive understanding of enigmas, dark sayings, hard sentences, secret things, time and seasons, understanding of your election, mandate and your Kingdom purpose on Earth. It is the clear knowledge of the redemptive purpose of the Son of God that was given to us, He who carries the government on His shoulders, whose name is called Wonderful, Counsellor, Mighty God and the Savior of the world.

Revelation is the shining of light into your inner thoughts for clear understanding of the perfect will of God and the mind of Christ to dominate your inheritance.

"I keep asking that the God of our Lord Jesus Christ, the glorious Father, may give you the Spirit[a] of wisdom and revelation, so that you may know him better. 18 I pray that the eyes of your heart may be enlightened in order that you may know the hope to which he has called you, the riches of his glorious inheritance in his holy people, 19 and his

incomparably great power for us who believe. That power is the same as the mighty strength 20 he exerted when he raised Christ from the dead and seated him at his right hand in the heavenly realms, 21 far above all rule and authority, power and dominion, and every name that is invoked, not only in the present age but also in the one to come." – Ephesians 1:17-21

Revelation brings you to the place and power of dominion. You will not be able to dominate what you do not understand. You cannot be in charge of a domain that you do not know clearly and understand intuitively. Dominion has boundaries. Revelation brings you to the place of prominence and the horizon of the fullness of your inheritance on Earth.

MANIFESTING YOUR REVELATION KNOWLEDGE

Without revelation, purpose is defeated.

When a revelation is released to you, the revelation must be manifested at the right time and season. For you to receive a revelation that will enhance your manifestation as a son of God there is a need for proper discerning and interpretation to unlock the prophetic promise in the revelation. You can only maximise the use of a product you clearly understand the purpose in the mind of the manufacturer for making the product.

After Mordecai got a revelation of the mind of God for the Jews and their inheritance, he was able to motivate Esther as the queen to do the right thing on the throne to deliver the Jews from destruction. Mordecai came to this place of prominence through the revelation he had about his purpose in the kings' palace. Revelation brings promotion.

"Mordecai the Jew was second in rank to King Xerxes, preeminent among the Jews, and held in high esteem by his many fellow Jews, because he worked for the good of his people and spoke up for the welfare of all the Jews." – Esther 10:3 (NIV)

A clear revelation is crucial to give you access to the secrets of the Lord. Revelation brings you to the place of authority and power. Everyone needs a revelation to dominate their territory.

"The secret things belong to the Lord our God, but the things revealed belong to us and to our children forever, that we may follow all the words of this law." – Deuteronomy 29:29 (NIV)

Dominion is a matter of ruling, reigning, subduing kingdoms, and dominating. It means taking up your Kingdom inheritance. Dominion is a matter of ruling on your throne. There is no throne without a kingdom, no kingdom without a king, no king without a domain. You cannot rule and dominate without the revelation and understanding of the Kingdom.

A RENEWED MIND

A fresh revelation of the majesty of God's kingdom will only come to a believer who has a renewed mind and a consecrated heart. The mind must be renewed, refashioned and repositioned to be able to process the eternal Kingdom purpose of God on Earth.

"Therefore, I urge you, brothers and sisters, in view of God's mercy, to offer your bodies as a living sacrifice, holy and pleasing to God—this is your true and proper worship. Do not conform to the pattern of this world, but be transformed by the renewing of your mind. Then you will be able to test and approve what God's will is—his good, pleasing and perfect will." – Romans 12:1-2 (NIV)

The mind must be rewired to be able to process and receive a fresh spiritual revelation meant to take you to the glory dimension where you will be able to rule, reign, subdue principalities and dominate the earth to the glory of God.

Revelation brings transformation. Transformation requires giving up the old wine skin for a new one. It is imperative that you overcome the work of the flesh, faulty mindsets, evil imaginations, worldly thoughts and conformity to the worldly system and traditions of men.

God wants to enlarge your vision include revelation of deep and secret things, the height and the width of the fullness of God's sovereign identity in order to comprehend His strategies and partnership with Him to complete His redemptive purpose on Earth.

God's Kingdom revelation will only come to a transformed mind, a contrite heart, with brokenness, humility, love, compassion, and a deep desire to surrender to the sovereign will of God.

"My sacrifice, O God, is a broken spirit; a broken and contrite heart you, God, will not despise." – Psalm 51:17

SANCTIFICATION

Sanctification requires revelation. When you have a revelation knowledge of the word of God, you will always live a sanctified life. You can consecrate yourself daily by the word of the Lord, for the word is life and truth. You grow up spiritually when you have a true revelation of the word of God.

The level of your revelation knowledge will determine your spiritual maturity, growth, conduct and strength of character. In other words, revelation enhances your growing up.

FAULTLESS FOUNDATION

"For look, the wicked bend their bows; they set their arrows against the strings to shoot from the shadows at the upright in heart. When the foundations are being destroyed, what can the righteous do?" – Psalm 11: 2-3 (NIV)

Living on the planet without a clear revelation of your Kingdom identity as a Godly ordained king and priest who is meant to reign on earth, is like sheep in the grave that death feeds on.

"Man that is in honour, and understandeth not, is like the beasts that perish." – Psalm 49:20 (KJV)

"They are like sheep and are destined to die; death will be their shepherd (but the upright will prevail over them in the morning). Their forms will decay in the grave, far from their princely mansions. But God will redeem me from the realm of the dead; he will surely take me to himself." – Psalm 49:14-15 (NIV)

Your personal foundational deliverance is complete when you are able to receive a clear revelation of your Kingdom dominion from the Throne of God.

"You have made them to be a kingdom and priests to serve our God, and they will reign on the earth." – Revelation 5:10

There is a need for deliverance from the power of the grave that mostly originates from faulty foundations. The grave

14

spirit is the spirit of captivity, limitation, fear and ignorance. The grave spirit is the spirit that swallows potential and puts your glory in complete obscurity. Your personal faulty foundation deliverance is complete when the eyes of your understanding supernaturally open to get a revelation that will enable you to rule, reign, subdue principalities and dominate the earth to the glory of God.

Deliverance from the captivity of the mighty causes you to experience an intuitive understanding of your Kingdom purpose and dominion. Jesus had to contend with the devil, the terrible one who has taken captive the glory of the saints and their kingdom dominion through the influence of the sins of Adam and Eve at the Garden of Eden.

This is why Jesus rose from the dead, ascended and led us out of captivity. He gave gifts unto men for the perfection of the body of Christ, equipping of the saints and completion of His redemptive purposes on Earth.

"But to each one of us grace has been given as Christ apportioned it. This is why it says: "When he ascended on high, he took many captives and gave gifts to his people." – Ephesians 4:7-8

Revelation of what Jesus has accomplished inside the grave before He ascended and gave gifts and grace unto men, is necessary for you to access your delegated authority and the grace He has earned for you. When you receive revelation of your Kingdom identity and dominion, you will no longer lose any battle and neither would you fall again for less!

Before Peter received the revelation, his lack of understanding and small faith was a concern for Jesus. Humans are always encumbered with the things of the flesh, doctrine, cultural mindset and the traditions of men.

"But what about you?" he asked. "Who do you say I am?" Simon Peter answered, "You are the Messiah, the Son of the living God." Jesus replied, "Blessed are you, Simon son of Jonah, for this was not revealed to you by flesh and blood, but by my Father in heaven." – Matthew 16:15-17

Jesus called Peter blessed after he identified Jesus as the Son of the living God and said to him that flesh and blood could not have made that revelation. The revelation had to come from His Father, the highest God.

"So I say, walk by the Spirit, and you will not gratify the desires of the flesh. For the flesh desires what is contrary to the Spirit and the Spirit what is contrary to the flesh. They are in conflict with each other, so that you are not to do whatever you want. But if you are led by the Spirit, you are not under the law." – Galatians 5:19-21 (NIV).

The Kingdom of God is not eating and drinking but righteousness and peace and joy in the Holy Spirit. Revelation will only come by paying the sacrifice of consecration and intimacy with Jesus, obedience to His counsel, the terms and conditions of the covenant relationship we have with the Father. There must be inner hunger and thirst for righteousness.

The revelation of the Kingdom of God and dominion brings inner joy – the joy that comes through the Holy Spirit and brings peace and strength.

"Nehemiah said, "Go and enjoy choice food and sweet drinks, and send some to those who have nothing prepared. This day is holy to our Lord. Do not grieve, for the joy of the Lord is your strength." – Nehemiah 8:10 (NIV)

The revelation of the kingdom brings inner peace in the realm of the Spirit. The Hebrew word for peace is shalom and it means "soundness".

"The fruit of that righteousness will be peace; its effect will be quietness and confidence forever." – Isaiah 32:17

A consecrated heart is the dwelling place of the fullness of the Holy Spirit. The Holy Spirit is the revealer of the secrets of the Kingdom. He is the executor of the Kingdom of God on Earth. Without the fullness of the Holy Spirit, there is not a clear revelation of the Kingdom of God. However, we speak the wisdom of God in a mystery, the hidden wisdom that God ordained before the ages for our glory, which none of the rulers of this age knew, for had they known they would not have crucified the Lord of glory.

"But we speak the wisdom of God in a mystery, the hidden wisdom which God ordained before the ages for our glory, 8 which none of the rulers of this age knew; for had they known, they would not have crucified the Lord of glory. But as it is written: "Eye has not seen, nor ear heard, Nor have entered into the heart of man The things which God has prepared for those who love Him." But God has revealed them to us through His Spirit. For the Spirit searches all things, yes, the deep things of God." – 1 Corinthians 2:7-10

We need a revelation of the deep things of the Kingdom of God in order to fulfil our Kingdom destiny. After Jesus ascertained that the disciples had understood the revelation of His Godly identity, He began to unfold to them a deeper revelation of His redemptive purpose on Earth.

He also gave a very important promise to give them the keys of the Kingdom of Heaven to exercise dominion and their delegated authority to rule, reign, subdue principalities and powers in the air and dominate the earth to the glory of God the Father.

STRATEGIC OPERATIONAL PRINCIPLES

- When God visited the disciples by the power of His Holy Spirit, they got a revelation of the splendour of His glory.

- Revelation generates bright light,

- Revelation gives unspeakable joy and peace that transcend human understanding. Get understand! Get revelation!

- Revelation gives you understanding of the significance of the times and seasons in your life journey.

- Revelation gives you authority and power to set boundaries and resist the devil at all times.

- Revelation enables you to rise above fear, frustrations, despair, depression and discouragement.

- Revelation gives you confidence and boldness to dominate your kingdom inheritance and possess the gates of the enemies of God.

- Revelation gives you access to draw grace from the throne of grace at the time of need.

- Revelation enhances your faith and makes your mountain to stand strong.

- Renew your mind daily and keep your heart with all diligence.

- Ask daily for the baptism of the fullness of the Holy Spirit.

- Ask daily for the baptism of the Spirit of revelation.

- Without revelation, purposes are defeated and destinies will be truncated!

- Without revelation you will be dominated and fall for less than your God given portion.

- Go beyond celebrating Jesus as a child that was born to us at Christmas. Move to the realm of a son that was given to us as the kingdom, the king of the kingdom that carries the government upon his shoulders and sits upon the throne of David to re-order the kingdom, establish righteousness and justice, the King whose kingdom will never come to an end.

CHAPTER 3

KINGDOM DOMINION

"Then to Him was given dominion and glory and a kingdom that all peoples, nations, and languages should serve Him. His dominion is an everlasting dominion, which shall not pass away. And His kingdom the one which shall not be destroyed."
Daniel 7:14

"Then the kingdom and dominion, and the greatness of the kingdom under the whole heaven, shall be given to the people, the saints of the Most High, His kingdom is an everlasting kingdom, and all dominions shall serve and obey Him." Daniel 7:27

The mandate of dominion is the Kingdom mandate to dominate all God's work on Earth. Dominion is sovereignty, having control over something, being in charge.

Dominion is a matter of ruling, reigning, subduing and taking back your stolen glory and the power that is your Kingdom inheritance. There is no Kingdom without a throne and there is no throne without a king and priest. There is no inheritance without holy priesthood. Dominion starts at the throne and understanding how to dominate from the throne is imperative.

"And have made us kings and priests to our God; and we shall reign on the earth." Revelation 5:10

After God created man in His own image and made them male and female, God saw that all what He has made was very good. Afterwards God blessed them, and said to them to be fruitful, multiply, fill the earth and subdue it, have dominion over the fish of the see, over the bird of the air, and over every living thing that moves on the earth. God even gave Adam the authority to name all the animals He created.

"Then God saw everything that He had made, and indeed it was very good. So the evening and the morning were the sixth day." Genesis 1:31

After God created man to act like Him and dominate the earth on His behalf to His glory, He finished His work and rested on the seventh day. He gave all the work of His hands to be managed by man and man was to rule, reign and subdue kingdoms and dominate the work of God's hands to show forth His glory.

In these last days, believers in Christ Jesus are not going to minister only by the anointing but by the glory of God. For this reason, God created man to dominate and manifest the glory of His kingdom on the planet. Little wonder that He made man to be a little lower than the angels and covered man with glory and honour.

"When I consider the heavens, the work of Your fingers, The moon and the stars, which You have ordained, What is man that You are mindful of him, And the son of man that You visit him? For you have made him a little lower than the angels, and You have crowned him with glory and honor." Psalm 8:3-5

"You have made him to have dominion over the works of Your hands; You have put all things under his feet." Psalm 8:6

PROGRESSIVE REVELATION TO DOMINATE THE EARTH

Progressive revelation through the Holy Spirit equips you with an inner strength to dominate your inheritance. You have dominion over what God reveals to you. The revelation knowledge that you possess, brings you to the place of dominion.

Satan attacks you in areas in which you actually lack revelation knowledge. No wonder the scriptures says God's people perish due to lack of revelation knowledge. You are vulnerable in areas where you lack progressive revelation knowledge and clear understanding.

Progressive revelation sheds light and dispels darkness. Lack of revelation knowledge brings confusion, despair and destruction. You can only exercise dominion through the revealed knowledge of God the Father of light.

Ironically, a professor of medicine or a pulmonary surgeon will be addicted to nicotine that eventually leads to lung cancer and sudden death. Lack of progressive revelation knowledge amounts to ignorance and spiritual blindness.

You may be blind to your entire Kingdom inheritance and benefits when you do not have access to progressive revelation in the light of the word of God through the Holy Spirit.

"My people are destroyed for lack of knowledge. Because you have rejected knowledge, I also will reject you from being priest for Me; because you have forgotten the law of your God, I also will forget your children. Hosea 4:6

Ignorance is a deadly weapon used by the devil to steal, kill and destroy the people of God! "My people are destroyed" The heirs of the kingdom are destroyed because of ignorance. Ignorance is being uninformed and having a lack of understanding about a particular subject.

A lack of revelation knowledge leaves people vulnerable to demonic strongholds and afflictions in the mind, spirit, soul and body. When you lack proper understanding of a particular subject, you can easily be dominated by error, assumptions and presumptions, which are sins before God. Lack of understanding can easily lead the people of God to compromise and be complacent.

"Who can understand his errors? Cleanse me from secret faults, keep back your servant also from presumptuous sins; let them not have dominion over me' then I shall be blameless, and I shall be innocent of great transgression." Psalm 19:12-13 (NKJV)

When you are dominated by presumptuous sins and secret faults, you will be devoid of revelation of secret and deep things from the heart of God.

"The secret things belong to the Lord our God, but those things which are revealed belong to us and to our children forever, that we may do all the words of the law." Deuteronomy 29:29

After Eli and his children departed from God's way, desecrating the temple of the Lord with abominable acts and immorality, God stopped speaking to Eli. He turned to the young Samuel and started revealing secret things to Samuel at the temple.

"Now the boy Samuel ministered to the LORD before Eli. And the word of the LORD was rare in those days; there was no widespread revelation. And it came to pass at that time, while

Eli, was lying down in his place, and when his eyes had begun to grow so dim that he could not see, and before the lamp of God went out in the tabernacle of the LORD where the ark of God was, and while Samuel was lying down, that the LORD called Samuel. And he answered, here I am! So he ran to Eli and said, here I am, for you called me. 1 Samuel 3:1-5 (NKJV).

Revelation comes through the fear of God and true intimacy with God. When you have the fear of God in your heart, you will be hungry and thirsty for righteousness; you will regard sins and unrighteousness as wickedness against God, like when Joseph was being tempted to commit adultery with Potiphar's wife. In resisting her he said, "My master has withheld nothing from me except you, because you are his wife. How then could I do such a wicked thing and sin against God?"

"And it came to pass after these things that his master's wife cast longing eyes on Joseph, and she said, "Lie with me." But he refused and said to his master's wife, Look, my master does not know what is with me in the house, and he has committed all that he has to my hand. There is no one greater in this house than I, nor has he kept back anything from me but you, because you are his wife. How then can I do this great wickedness, and sin against God?" Genesis 39:7-9

"The secret of the Lord is with them that fear Him; and he will shew them His covenant." Psalm 25:14

The Lord confides in those who fear Him and keeps His commandments and the terms of the covenant. Revelation knowledge gives right direction and delivers you from the snares of the fowlers.

STRATEGIC OPERATIONAL PRINCIPLES

- Dominion is kingdom imperative and spiritual warfare.

- The war we are fighting is the war of dominating our Kingdom inheritance that was stolen originally through sin of disobedience.

- Believers in Jesus Christ must learn how to dominate from the throne and kick Satan out of their domain and inheritance.

- Dominion is linked to boundaries. It is a finished and concluded war and God has set the boundaries.

- It is a war without physical weapons.

- It is a battle for our inheritance

- It is a battle of faith in the finished work on the Cross of Calvary.

- It is an imperative battle that we must fight to the end.

- It is a battle we must be well conversant with if we want to reign and rule with Jesus at His second coming to Judge the Earth!

- The sovereign God created man in His own image, likeness and characteristics to act like Him, to see like Him and to exercise authority on Earth and manage all that He created.

- God put Adam and Eve in the garden and gave Adam the keys to live in Eden and keep it and enjoy His presence and His goodness in the garden. When God placed Adam in Eden, He gave Him the operational principles to manage the garden as His kingdom dominion and to be in charge completely. God Almighty gave Adam everything to ensure a peaceful existence in the garden, including a helpmate as his companion.

"Then God said, Let Us make man in Our image, according to Our likeness; let them have dominion over the fish of the sea, over the birds of the air, and over the cattle, over all the earth and over every creeping thing that creeps on the earth. So God created man in His own image; in the image of God He created him; male and female He created them. Genesis 1:26-27

- We were created in God's image to establish dominion over nature and be in charge of creation and be fruitful, multiply, reign, rule subdue and dominate (Genesis 1:26-28).

- We were created to dominate Kingdoms as kings and priests to our God (Revelation 5:10).

- We were created to manage creation and dominate the earth by manifesting God's glory – not for creation to manage and dominate us and for sin to have dominion over us!

CHAPTER 4

THE KINGDOM KEYS

"And I also say to you that you are Peter, and on this rock I will build My church, and the GATES of hell shall not prevail against it. "And I will give you the KEYS of the KINGDOM of Heaven and whatsoever you bind on earth will be bound in heaven, and whatever you loose on earth will be loosed in heaven." Matthew 16:18-19

The Hebrew word for a key in Hebrew is called "maphteah", which means, "the opener". Keys are principles and law that you use diligently to access, dominate your inheritance, and become victorious in life.

The keys must be used with the right principles. Keys gives access, permission, authority, liberty and ability to enter a place. Keys gives freedom or ability to obtain and make use of valuable things.

keys gives access to the treasure of the king. It gives access to the hidden treasure of secret places to do His will and execute His counsels.

Keys are indispensable elements in getting whatever you need to function and fulfil your Kingdom purpose on Earth.

Keys are powerful instruments used to open the gates and have access to your inheritance and possessions. A key is a symbol of authority.

"The key of the house of David, I will lay on his shoulder; so he shall open, and no one shall shut; And he shall shut, and no one shall open." Isaiah 22:22

Keys are released to those who understand the operational strategies of the keys to effectively open and shut gates.

The Lord Jesus Christ descended to the lower part of the earth, He led captivity captive and set all things in order that sin has disordered. He collected back the keys of the Kingdom of heaven that Satan had stolen originally from Eden and delivered the keys into our hands to use, the keys based on the level of our understanding and revelation of the Kingdom and the revelation of His resurrection power.

Simon Peter answered and said, You are Christ, the Son of the living God. Jesus answered and said replied to him, "Blessed are you, Simon Bar-Jonah, for flesh and blood has not revealed this to you, but My Father who is in heaven." After Jesus ascertained the fact that the disciples had a revelation of who He is as Christ, the Son of the living God, who is carrying the government upon His shoulders, He now declared that He will give them the KEYS of the Kingdom of heaven to open the Throne gates and to rule and reign as kings and priests unto God.

A revelation gives you access to the keys of the Kingdom. Without a revelation, you will not be able to use the keys of the Kingdom effectively.

THE POWER OF KEYS

Keys are very important in gaining access to any place of operation and authority. Without keys, doors and gates cannot be opened.

The concept of the kingdom of God and our inheritance in the nations is aligned with the Church. The Church needs to understand how to operate the keys of the Kingdom to possess their Kingdom inheritance in the nations. If you understand the matter of the Kingdom and the importance of the keys of the Kingdom with the operational principles, then you will cooperate with God to work out your salvation with the delegated authority in unison by the power of the Holy Spirit.

THE VISION OF A BIG GOLDEN CROSS

My heart was burdened by the present situation of the Church in our generation, and seeing the kingdom of darkness prevailing against the Church in contrast to the promise and the assurance that Jesus gave the disciples after they got the revelation of His mysterious identity as Christ the son of the living God.

"And I also say to you that you are Peter, and on this rock I will build My church, and the GATES of hell shall not prevail against it."

I began to ask the Lord why the gates of Hell are prevailing against His church that He built upon the solid rock of Christ, the Son of the living God. And He showed me a massive palace with a very big golden cross at the gate of the palace, where there was perfect serenity. When l got to this heavenly palace, l heard a voice in the midst of the palace as l was asking in my mind: that "Where is this place?"

The voice came loudly: "This is the heavenly court where verdicts are taken, with the Trinity upon the Throne. The massive golden cross with the blood of the everlasting covenant that was shed on this cross is the key to My Throne and an evidence against the accuser of the brethren. I have given unto you the keys to come boldly to the Throne of grace and operate from this Throne with these keys as your inheritance and the seal of the covenant of the everlasting priesthood that I have made with you through the sacrifice of My blood. Unfortunately, My people who are called by My name, often complain and grumble instead of legislating at this Court of heaven, My Throne where the blood of the everlasting covenant is crying for mercy daily!"

Afterwards, the Lord began to reveal to me the seven keys of the Kingdom with the operational principles to rule, reign, subdue principalities and dominate our Kingdom inheritance on Earth to the glory of God.

These keys will be discussed in detail in this book, with the operational principles as it was downloaded to me from the throne of grace. God gave me clear instructions to write and publish the book for generations to read and be well informed on how to win the war that the kingdom of darkness is waging against the church of God, and to understand how to prevail against the gates of hell and dominate the inheritances of the saints in Christ Jesus.

THE KEYS OF THE KINGDOM

We have a Kingdom, and the keys that were purchased by the blood of Jesus to operate on the throne in the Kingdom. These seven Kingdom keys have been given unto believers in Christ Jesus to complete the work that Jesus did, the victory He accomplished by the power of His blood.

"I was watching, and the same horn was making war against the saints, and prevailing against them, until the ancient of days came and a judgement was made in favour of the saints of the Most High, and the time came for the saints to possess the kingdom." Daniel 7:21-22

Inasmuch as judgement has already been made in favor of the saints to possess the Kingdom, the saints have the responsibility to arise with these keys to subdue the kingdom of darkness, shine forth the glory of God and establish the Kingdom of God in the hearts of men, babes, kings, queens, people in authority and the nations of the world.

The seven Kingdom keys were purchased by the blood of Jesus to operate the principles of the Kingdom to reign and dominate the earth. Elisha got the keys from Elijah through sacrifice and focus, but unfortunately, no one was able to pay the sacrifice and get the keys from Elisha to operate in the supernatural. The Kingdom keys activate the power of God inside of you and enable you to become a supernatural being and terror to the kingdom of darkness. The keys of the Kingdom give you authority, access, ownership, control, freedom and power to operate on the throne and dominate your inheritance in the Kingdom.

THE KEYS OF THE HOUSE OF DAVID

"The keys of the house of David I will lay on his shoulder; So he shall open, and no one shall shut; And he shall shut, and no one shall open, I will fasten him as a peg in a secure place, and he will become a glorious throne to his father's house." Isaiah 22:22-23

Every kingdom has keys that are used to operate in the kingdom. God gave Adam the keys of dominion, to be fruitful, multiply and fill the earth.

The keys of the house of David are the keys to the Throne of God. The keys to the royal throne, the market thrones, the nation's thrones. The keys of David are the authority and power to open the gates to access the Kingdom inheritance upon the throne. They also close every gate of hell and death that hinders the fulfilment of the purposes of God on the throne. The keys of the house of David are used to dominate the Kingdom.

Satan manipulated the operational principles of the keys that God gave Adam and stole their inheritance. Keys are used to possess the gates of our inheritance and take hold of our possessions. Jesus Christ used the seven keys of the Kingdom to possess the Kingdom and restore the glory before He delivered the keys into the hands of the disciples with the delegated authority to use the keys to possess the gates of the enemies of God.

The keys of the house of David are the keys of the Kingdom to restore the glory of God and of His Kingdom.

STRATEGIC OPERATIONAL PRINCIPLES

- Ask God to open the eyes of your understanding and take you beyond positional truth to experiential truth through a revelation of the keys of the Kingdom and the operational principles. Ephesians 1:17-18.

- Keys are powerful instruments that open gates to your possessions.

- Keys give you access to your Kingdom inheritance and the benefits of the Kingdom.

- Keys are God's delegated authority that authorizes you to dominate the earth.

- Keys enable you to tap into the supernatural, endowing power, the gifts He has provided for us in the heavenly places to reign on Earth, fulfill your Kingdom destiny and reign with Him upon His throne as overcomers in the end.

- You must be in a covenant relationship with God and the Holy Spirit to receive the keys of the Kingdom.

- The keys are a priceless gift of the Kingdom to open the prison doors to those who are bound, to operate on the throne of grace.

- Keys of the Kingdom are released unto the overcomers, those who are determined to run without fainting, the warriors who overcome evil with good, those who hold on to God's words without wavering.

- Keys of the kingdom are released to those who treasured the word of God and do not deny His name in times of adversity and trials.

- Keys of the Kingdom are released to those who have obedient and humble hearts. Those who obey God's commandments. They will receive the keys to set the captives free and loose the band of wickedness.

- Keys of the Kingdom are released unto the overcomers who keep their eyes from doing evil and their tongues from slandering. Those who will see with the eyes of the Spirit and are ready to speak on God's behalf.

CHAPTER 5

THE POWER OF GATES

Gates represent access to authority and the seat of power. The king has a throne at the gates. The elders often sit at the gates to make decisions and pass judgement. Gates are spiritual. Gates does not move, but the plan and God's expectation is that the Church must smash the gates of Hell. Gates are places where important decisions are taken.

Strongmen can be at gates in a city or nation as gatekeepers. Important decisions that involve life and death are taken at the gates. Businesses are established at the gates. Elders and Prophets of God stood at the gates of the city to make declarations from the Lord. Kings sat at the gates to dispense judgement.

"For a Spirit of justice to him who sits in judgement, And for strength to those who turn back the battle at the gate". Isaiah 28:6

"You shall appoint judges and officers in all your gates, which the LORD your God gives you, according to your tribes, and they shall judge the people with judgement". – Deuteronomy 16:18.

GATES ARE SPIRITUAL

Gates are powerful forces and supernatural entities that give access to the possessions of an everlasting inheritance.

Gates are significant phenomena in life, which need special understanding to move to the next level in life. God gave Abraham a promise in Genesis that he will possess the gates of his enemy and dominate his inheritance. Jesus also promised the disciples that He would give them the keys of the Kingdom, and that the gates of Hell shall not prevail against His church.

"That in blessing I will bless thee, and in multiplying I will multiply thy seed as the stars of the heaven and as the sand which is upon the sea shore; and thy seed shall possess the gate of his enemies." – Genesis 22:17

"And I also say to you that you are Peter, and on this rock I will build My church, and the gates of Hell shall not prevail against it." – Matthew 16:18

A gate is a doorway to authority. A gate is an entry point and departure point. A gate is a major element that determines the level of your possessions and productivity. A gate will not move without the right KEY! Little wonder that Jesus emphasized consecration in **Psalm 24:3-6** before He dealt with gates in verses *7-10* for Him to be able to move and complete His Redemptive assignment!

"Who shall ascend into the hill of the Lord? Or who shall stand in his holy place? He that hath clean hands, and a pure heart; who hath not lifted up his soul unto vanity, nor sworn deceitfully, He shall receive the blessing from the Lord, and righteousness from the God of his salvation. This is the generation of them that seek him that seek thy face, O Jacob." Psalm 24:3-6

There are gates that must be lifted in your life before you can actually access the throne of grace and fulfil your Kingdom destiny. Jesus had to deal with different gates and ancient doors before He could collect the keys of the Kingdom, and access the legal authority and power that He handed over to as many that believe in Him and accepted Him as their personal Lord and Saviour. We must use the keys to rule, reign, subdue principalities and powers in high places and dominate the earth and restore His glory.

"Lift up your heads, O ye gates; and be ye lift up, ye everlasting doors; and the King of glory shall come in. Who is this King of glory? The Lord strong and mighty, the Lord mighty in battle. Lift up your heads, O ye gates; even lift them up, ye everlasting doors; and the King of glory shall come in. who is this King of glory? The Lord of hosts, he is the King of glory." Psalm 24:7-10

Gates can hear the spoken word because they are spiritual entities. Jesus ordered the gates to be lifted with the authority and power of His word for Him to gain access to fulfil His redemptive purpose on the earth.

TYPES OF GATES

There are different types of gates mentioned in the word of God with significant characteristics. There are physical, spiritual, commercial, political and institutional gates. We have to discern the gates in our cities and where they are located by using the power of the Holy Spirit. We need to discern the strongmen and the gatekeepers that operate at these gates. Gates have security guards that give signals to those strongmen that operate at the gates. We need divine wisdom and the keys of the Kingdom to deal with gates. Every satanic false altar raised in the market places, institutions, road junctions, the city entrances, hospitals and the nation's boarders are gates of Hell where the souls of men are tied and blood sacrifice is being made regularly with demonic activities going on at the gates.

THE GATES OF RIGHTEOUSNESS

The gates of righteousness are strait and holy. It is a narrow way that leads unto life, and few people are found at the gates
of righteousness. Many people find it difficult to enter the gates of righteousness because of deccitfulness of sins and the lust of the flesh. The gates of righteousness will only be open to the people that walk in truth and holiness unto the Lord. The faithful people who do what pleases the heart of God.

"Open to me the gates of righteousness; I will go through them, And I will praise the LORD. This is the gate of the LORD, through which the righteous shall enter." – Psalm 118:19-20

"Open the gates that the righteous nation which keeps the truth may enter in." – Isaiah 26:2

Those who are qualified to enter the gates of righteousness, will be kept in the perfect peace of God, they will have access to all the benefits of God's Kingdom. They will find rest, abundant life and dwell in the light and safety all their days.

The qualifications to enter the gates of righteousness are:

- Keeping the truth of the word of God without compromise.

44

- Complete obedience to the Gospel of the Kingdom of God.

- Becoming the son of God by faith in Jesus Christ.

- Total separation from sins, iniquity and the works of the flesh.

The gates of righteousness are always open to those who will trust the Lord Jesus Christ. They never closed for the mercies of the Lord. You find grace at the time of need at the gates of righteousness. The gates of righteousness are the gates of restoration.

THE GATE OF PRAISES

"…..But you shall call your walls salvation, and your gates Praise." Isaiah 60:18

"Enter into his gates with thanksgiving and into His courts with praises: be thankful unto him, and bless his name." – Psalm 100:4

"Blessed are they that do His commandments that they may have right to the tree of life, and may enter in through the gates into the city." – Revelation 22:14

The gates of New Jerusalem are called praise because gates speak of entrance, and all who enter into this glorious city will sing endless praises to God. All who come to the city will praise God for all that He has done. Those who are helped by the city will praise God for His goodness, His mercy, and His love. When all creation beholds the city, it will rejoice and praise God. New Jerusalem is a city of praise because only the conquerors will be able to enter through the gates to the city and their mouths will be filled with praises and thanksgiving. Praises and thanksgiving are offered as sacrifices at the gate of the City.

THE GATES OF HEAVEN

"The Lord loveth the gates of Zion more than all the dwellings of Jacob." – Psalm 87:2

Gates are very significant and do not move, but the Church must move with boldness and in righteousness to operate and control the gates in the nations.

In this fullness of time, we need to have a clear understanding of the keys of the Kingdom that Jesus Christ earned with His blood with the tremendous work He did inside the grave. He rose victoriously after leading captivity captive and gave us the keys with the gift of His unlimited grace before He ascended. He now sits at the right hand of

God Almighty, making intercession for us and waiting until the present ruler of this world becomes our footstool.

"Go through, Go through the gates! Prepare the way for the people, Build up the highway! Take out the stones, Lift up a banner for the people!" Isaiah 62:10.

"Open the gates that the righteous nation which keeps the truth may enter in". – Isaiah 26:2.

"In that day the Lord of Host will be for a crown of glory and a diadem of beauty To the remnant of His people, For a spirit of justice to him who sits in judgement, And strength to those who turn back the battle at the gate." – Isaiah 28:5-6

It is time for the righteous to arise at this fullness of time to begin to possess the gates and take back our Kingdom inheritance in the cities and nations by the keys of the Kingdom with our delegated authority.

Jacob went from being unaware of God's presence, to vibrantly aware of God in His midst upon waking from his dream, where angels ascended and descended a ladder from Heaven to Earth. Jacob was afraid after he had a night vision.

"And Jacob awaked out of his sleep, and he said, surely the Lord is in this place; and I knew it not. And he was afraid, and said, How dreadful is this place! This is none other but the house of God, and this is the gate of heaven." – Genesis 28:16-17

Jacob was the first personality in scripture to commemorate his encounter with God by remembering the place where it occurred. The word "House of God" is the altar of God, a dwelling place where life and worship abound, a place of prayers and where intercessions goes up to the almighty God, a meeting point with the Trinity. Jacob described the house of God as "the gate of heaven".

The encounter Jacob had at "Luz" which he later named "Bethel" after his vivid encounter with God, described gates as a transitional place, in this case a connection point between Heaven and Earth, where Heaven's activity touched Earth and God's presence changed the spiritual and natural realm. Jacob's dream caused a shift in his mind-set that changed his perspectives about God's presence. Wherever an altar is being raised unto God, it represents a gate to the throne of His majesty.

"And Jacob vowed a vow, saying, if God will be with me, and will keep me in this way that I go, and will give me bread to eat, and raiment to put on. So that I come again to my father's house in peace; then shall the Lord be my God, and this stone, which I have set for a pillar, shall be God's house and of all that thou shalt give me I will surely give the tenth unto thee." – Genesis 28:20-22

A gate is a place of divine transaction, a connecting point where vows are made.

The gates of Heaven are meeting point with God where there is light and perfection. It is a place of covenant where there is an exchange of vows. It is a place where divine transformation takes place with covenant blessings from God. The gate of Heaven is where mercy and manifold grace are released. A church or sanctuary is a gate of Heaven. Any place where an altar is raised unto Almighty represents a gate of Heaven.

THE GATES OF HELL

The gates of Hell are the territory of destruction and darkness. The gates of Hell are the gates of the grave, which is broader road than the gates of Heaven, because they lead to destruction through the deceitfulness of sin. Iniquities and wickedness, disobedience, unforgiveness, witchcraft, addiction, selfishness, idolatry, pride, false religion, sexual perversion, lies and the likes are the foundation of the gates of Hell.

Many go in at the gate because it seems right unto them; Satan makes it look right through the covering of darkness and lack of knowledge and revelation.

"There is a way that seems right to a man, But its end is the way of death." – Proverbs 16:25

The gates of Hell have a mandate to scatter the Church and put people into bondage with the covering of darkness. Because the church has been given the keys of the Kingdom, the gates of Hell shall not prevail because the Lord Jesus Christ Himself has prevailed and collected the keys of the Kingdom from Satan and delivered it into the hands of the righteous. With the keys, we can set the captives free, proclaim liberty to the captives and open the prison doors to those who are bound. We can repair the ruined cities and raise up the desolate generations with these keys.

GATES OF RICHES

The treasures and riches of the earth have gates that need to be opened for believers to access the resources for the gospel of the Kingdom of God.

"Thus saith the Lord to His anointed, to Cyrus, whose right hand I have Holden, to subdue nations before him; and I will lose the loins of the kings, to open before him the two leaved gates; and the gates shall not be shut; I will go before thee, and make the crooked places straight: I will break in pieces the gates of brass, and cut in sunder the bars of iron: And I will give thee the treasures of darkness, and hidden riches of secret places, that thou mayest know that I, the Lord, which call thee by thy name, am the God of Israel." – Isaiah 45:1-3

Access to wealth and riches could be gained through these spiritual gates. The gates need the right keys to be opened. The devil also operates at these gates when the gates are opened unto him through sins and iniquities, which gives him authority to access and steal the inheritance of the saints.

PERSONAL LIFE GATES

The personal life gates represent an entrance into your life that can be left vulnerable to attack from the devil through sins and iniquities. The gates of your life can be loved by God or hated through whatever you allow to come into your life. There are gates that control every operational management in the spiritual realm. If there is no access through the gates of your life, it will be virtually impossible for demonic forces and evil spirit to come into your life.

Types of life gates;
- The heart gate
- The eyes gate
- The ear gate
- The mouth gate
- The private organ gate

"My son, attend to my words; incline thine ear unto my sayings. Let them not depart from thine eyes; keep them in the midst of thine heart." – Proverbs 4:20-21

"Keep your heart with all diligence; for out of it are the issues of life. Put away from thee a forward mouth, and perverse lips put far from thee. Let thine eyes look right on, and let thine eyelids look straight before thee." – Proverbs 4:23-25

THE HEART – The heart gathers dust through what we allow into it. You have control over the gates of your heart. The heart gates can be opened to the devil through evil thoughts, evil imaginations, evil counsel, corrupt communication, evil perceptions, faulty mindset, evil jealousy, bitterness, hatred, anger, pride and unforgiveness.

THE EYES – The eyes are the gates to the soul and spirit. The gates of the eyes might be opened to lust through what you see. Pornography is an evil spirit that destroys the saints of God easily through the gate of the eyes (watching). A whole family was under the influence of satanic oppression through pornography for almost two years with serious affliction that promised to kill and destroy, until the Holy Spirit led the mother of the young boy to my husband and myself to minster to the whole family.

Pornography is an evil spirit of destruction and when you open, the gates of your eyes once to a pornographic site on the internet or you watch a video that is it! The spirits with all the gatekeepers will never let you go, even for one day, without visiting the site until you are destroyed if there is no-one to minister deliverance to you!

THE EARS – The gates of your ears will be opened to evil spirits through what you listen to; gossip, backstabbing, busybodies and worldly music that corrupt good intentions.

THE PRIVATE ORGAN – The private part of every human being is a very powerful gate. It is a place of covenant that you must guard jealously. When you open this gate through sexual intercourse, you will be under the influence of any spirits that control the person that you have intercourse with, which affect all areas of your life, including your destiny.

Illegitimate sexual intercourse with someone you are not legally married to will open the gate of your life to evil spirits and will make you vulnerable to the gate of Hell to prevail against your life and dominate your inheritance.

When gates are established, it can no longer move on its own unless someone moves it with the right keys. Gates have gatekeepers that watch over the gates as security guards who monitor everything that enters and leaves through the gates.

God will rejoice over your life through the holy things that you allow into your life gates (Zephaniah 3:16-17). You cannot prevail against the gates of Hell if you do not know how to guard the gates of your life jealously.

It is imperative to be vigilant about denying access to the devil to prevail against the gates of our lives by regularly avoiding verbal discourse or dialogue with the devil through his subtle distractions.

POSSESSING THE GATES

He that possesses the right keys to control the gates determines the fate of those who dwell within the city and determines what goes into the city. Possessing the gates of the enemy is prevailing against all the attacks from the kingdom of darkness to dominate your inheritance.

Jesus Christ diligently dealt with the gates of Hell and dispelled darkness so that He could fulfill His redemptive purpose on Earth without constraint and hindrance.

Complete obedience to God's commandments and determinate counsels will give you the boldness and confidence to use the keys of the Kingdom to rule, reign, subdue principalities and powers and dominate your Kingdom inheritance.

If you open the gate of your heart unto bitterness and unforgiveness, you have invited paranoia spirits to enter in and torment your life and the enemy will possess the gates of your life instead of you possessing his gates.

When Nehemiah finished the work of restoration by building the wall of Jerusalem, except for installing the doors of the gates of the city, Satan used Sanballat, Tobiah and Geshem to devise evil schemes to hinder Nehemiah through major distractions, conspiracy and physical threats. The devil often roams about like a roaring lion to seek for open gates in a believer's life to enter and cause them to lose their Kingdom focus and hinder the fulfilment of their Kingdom destiny.

Nehemiah did not lose his Kingdom focus. He discerned Satan's strategy and the gates that Satan wanted to use to distract and hinder him from completing the work. You need the fullness of the Holy Spirit to discern the devil's tactics and to know people in the spirit.

"That in blessing I will bless thee, and in multiplying I will multiply thy seed as the stars of the heaven and as the sand which is upon the sea shore; and thy seed shall possess the gate of his enemies." – Genesis 22:17

"And they blessed Rebekah, and said unto her, Thou art out sister, be thou the mother of thousands of millions, and let thy seed possess the gate of those which hate them." – Genesis 24:60

The Lord blessed Abraham, promised to multiply his seed, and give his seed the keys to possess the gates of His enemies. Rebekah was also blessed by her kinsmen before she was released to her husband to go and bear seed that will possess the gates of their enemies. All our children in their generation are supposed to possess the gates of the enemies of God because out of their mouths the Lord has ordained strength and made them as arrows and keys in our hands to possess the gates of the enemies and prevail against the gates of Hell.

Although our children have been ordained from the womb to possess the gates of their enemies and the enemies of our God, it is the responsibility of the parents to pay particular attention to the mentoring and discipleship of the children.

Your children should be your first congregants and mentees. If your discipleship and mentorship does not work at home, you must not export it! The glory of your children must be restored first before you restore other people's glory. Leadership starts from leading yourself effectively before you lead others.

It is quite imperative to begin to teach children the rudiments of spiritual warfare as babes, because they are designed to be arrows and new threshing instruments that are kept in God's quiver and are dished out by God as He deems, fit to subdue the kingdom of darkness and dominate the earth to His glory.

David, as a young lad, defeated Goliath and possessed the gates of the enemies of God and the Israelites. He prevailed against the gate of Hell through the power of God that worked inside of him.

The gates of Hell are currently prevailing against the church after Jesus paid an expensive price for the keys of the Kingdom and delivered the keys to the Church, which He built upon the rock of His Kingdom identity as the victorious Son of the living God. He is the Saviour who died and rose to give us all the authority in Heaven and on the earth to rule, reign, subdue the kingdom of darkness and live victoriously as kings and priests.

This secret of having the understanding of our Kingdom identity, knowing who we are as kings and priest who are called to reign on Earth, is what Satan has been keeping from Christians throughout the centuries, so the Church will not rise to possess the gates of the enemies of God and have dominion over their Kingdom inheritance.

"To me, who am less than the least of all the saints, this grace was given, that I should preach among the Gentiles the unsearchable riches of Christ." – Ephesians 3:8
"And to make all see what is the fellowship of the mystery, which from the beginning of the ages has been hidden in God who created all things through Jesus Christ, to the intent that now the manifold wisdom of God might be made known by the church to the principalities and powers in the heavenly places, according to the eternal purpose which He accomplished in Christ Jesus our Lord." – Ephesians 3:9-11

"In whom we have boldness and access with confidence through faith in Him." – Ephesians 3:12

The life-changing apostolic prayers that Paul prayed in Ephesians 3:17-19 and Colossians 1:9-14 are keys for building strong spiritual foundations that will enable the saints of God to fulfill the responsibility of proclaiming the manifold wisdom of God and the power of His resurrection, which He accomplished in Christ Jesus our Lord, to the principalities and powers in heavenly places.

I pray these prayers most often for myself until l see the manifestation in my life and l taught my children to pray these apostolic prayers into their lives regularly for them to be able to fulfill their Kingdom purpose on Earth.

SECURING YOUR GATES

The gate is a stronghold and a supernatural phenomenon; standards are lifted at the gates. The banners are lifted up for the people at the gates. The gates must be guarded diligently and purified, because they determine what goes into your life.

"And he set gatekeepers at the gates of the house of the Lord, so that no one who was in any way unclean should enter." 2 Chronicles 23:19

The priests and the elders have to secure the gates and determine what goes in and what comes out. This is because gates represent the place of authority and entrance into the heart of the city. The priests and the elders are to operate the gates because they are full of wisdom, understanding and the knowledge of what constitute their inheritance and domain.

Every domain has boundaries and understanding the boundaries of their domain will enable them to make decisions at the gate and make sure there is no adversary or anyone who does not have the legal right to be there. Only those possessing the keys will be able to enter the heart of the city to possess and dominate their Kingdom inheritance.

Jesus Christ secured the gates and dealt with the gates of Hell for Him to fulfil His redemptive purpose on Earth. Jesus used the keys of the Kingdom to command the gates to be lifted for the passage of the King of Kings to restore the glory and power of His Kingdom.

"Lift up your heads, O you gates! And be lifted up, you everlasting doors! And the King of glory shall come in. Who is this King of glory? The Lord strong and mighty, The Lord mighty in battle. Lift up your heads, O you gates! Lift up, you everlasting doors! And the King of glory shall come in." – Psalm 24:7-10

Some gates must be lifted for your Kingdom destiny to be fulfilled and for you to manifest the glory and power of God in your generation. Every gate of your life you might have opened to the kingdom of darkness must also be identified and shut down completely with deep repentance for a season of forgiveness and refreshing to come upon you, to manifest your purpose and shine forth the glory of God.

The gates were opened for Joseph and he was able to move from the prison to the palace as he refused to compromise and defile himself. The Lord opened the gates to the throne for Esther; He destroyed all the satanic gatekeepers and their wicked machinations against the Jews for Esther to be able to fulfil her redemptive purpose on the throne as a Queen who saved her generation.

All the gates of wickedness and ancestral foundational gates must be closed for a new gate to be opened to fulfil your Kingdom purpose on Earth.

To release the treasure of darkness and the hidden riches of secret places to advance the gospel of the Kingdom as Kingdom financier, the amour of kings must be loosed and certain gates of bronze must be broken into pieces.

"I will go before thee, and make the crooked places straight: I will break in pieces the gates of brass, and cut in sunder the bars of iron: And I will give thee the treasures of darkness and hidden riches of secret places, that you may know that I, the LORD, who call you by your name, Am the God of Israel." Isaiah 45:3.

GUARD THE GATES OF YOUR HEART

"Keep your heart with all diligence, for out of it spring the issues of life." – Proverbs 4:23

Different thoughts – good and evil – that flow from the heart, evil imaginations and evil jealousy that flow from the heart through what you hear, feel, see and imagine affect your heart gates. All evil thoughts and imaginations block the gate to the throne of grace and make you vulnerable to sin and unrighteousness that produce fear.

Elijah was gripped with fear after a major defeat and ran for his life into a cave after satanic confrontation with Ahab and Jezebel. Elijah allowed what he heard and saw to create fear in his heart, which led to him, the prophet of restoration, to run and hide in a cave. Jezebel locked the Man of God out of the throne room of grace into a cave where he was tormented with fear, depression, discouragement and despair.

God later gave Elijah prophetic instructions to get out of the cave of discouragement and vulnerability and come to the throne of grace where he could access the strength of God and receive fresh anointing. You have to set boundaries for the devil. Your domain has holy boundaries and gates to keep evil out. When you open the gates of your domain and the gates of your life to the devil through sin and iniquities, you give Satan permission to cross your boundaries and steal your authority and Kingdom inheritance.

It is imperative to guard jealously the gate of your heart and keep the boundaries of your domain from all unrighteous acts and iniquities.

STRATEGIC OPERATIONAL PRINCIPLES

"And on this ROCK I will build my church and the gates of hell shall not prevail against it. And I will give you the KEYS of the KINGDOM of HEAVEN, and whatsoever you bind on earth will be bound in Heaven." – Matthew 16: 18-19.

- We are God's living Church, created for His purpose to reign, rule, subdue the kingdom of darkness and dominate the earth to the glory of God's name.

- I acknowledge God's sovereignty over my life, I thank God for His wisdom and the gift of the keys of the Kingdom to open every gate to claim and dominate my stolen inheritance.

- I repent through the blood of Jesus of every gate that I might have opened in my life to give Satan access to dominate my Kingdom inheritance.

- I confess, repent and renounce every gate that has been opened in my life through my ancestors and all the altars in my body through incisions, tattoos, witchdoctors' incantations and consultations to false altars and false prophets.

- In Jesus name, I shut down every gate of death, limitation, failure, stagnancy, calamity, poverty, perversion and other evil occurrences that have been opened in my life.

- I Command every door that has been closed over my business, academic career, my career and all my endeavors to open now by the fire in the blood of Jesus!

- I Command the gate of the word of God to open unto me now for deep revelation of the word of God.

- I command the gates of the wealth of the nations and the hidden riches of the secret places to open to me for the release of all the resources I need to fulfill my Kingdom mandate without limitations.

- As the King of glory enters into my present situation in my life, I declare that my glory will start to shine because my time has come to manifest the glory of God with glorious liberty!

- Lord, open to me the gates of righteousness. I will go through them and I will praise the Lord (Psalm 118:19).

- Lord, let not the gates of my life, family-calling election be desolate (Lamentations 1:4)

- Lord, subdue nation, strip kings of their armour, open doors, level mountains, break down gates of bronze and cut through bars of iron. Lord, I claim the hidden treasures and riches stored in secret places in Your name (Isaiah 45:1-3).

- Lord, open to me the gates of the nations and make me a banner of righteousness for my generation (Isaiah 26:2, Isaiah 62:10).

CHAPTER 6

THE KEY OF UNITY AND LOVE

"Again I say to you that if two of you agree on earth concerning anything that they ask, it will be done for them by My Father in heaven. For where two or three are gathered the together in My name, I am there in the midst of them." – Matthew 18:19-20

Unity means undivided attention and perfect agreement with one another. Unity is love without hypocrisy but bearing with one another in complete loyalty. The Greek word of agree is sumphoneo. Sum means "together", phoneo is to sound. Metaphorically the word means to agree together according to the word of God.

Agreement prayers unlock the supernatural. Agreement prayers together as a church, means a cooperative action and synergising together which unlock ancient and everlasting doors.

"Behold, how good and how pleasant it is for brethren to dwell together in UNITY! It is like the precious oil upon the head, running down on the beard, the beard of Aaron, running down

on the edge of his garments. It is like the dew of Hermon, descending upon the mountains of Zion; For there the Lord commanded the blessings, Life forevermore." – Psalm 133.

The word Hermon means "devoted", "sanctified" or "holy". Hermon was a majestic mountain, a fitting place to represent the presence of God and reveal the glory of God. Perfect unity and holy concord is as dew, mysteriously blessed. Unity is an unbroken strong alliance; unity is a powerful weapon and unbroken cord linking believers to the throne of grace. Unity draws mercy and brings down God's presence! There is tremendous anointing and strength in unity.

Whenever brotherly love abounds, where love reigns, God reigns there also. There God Himself commands His blessings and He is present there in the Spirit because God is LOVE. No, wonder that He gives His abundant blessings of eternal life and inheritance where love abounds, for love is life. Wherever the brethren dwell together in unity and love, the blessings and enjoyment of eternity start.

Unity brings an unprecedented anointing upon the body, which Satan cannot stand against! Where two or three are gathered in one accord, God reigns. The glory of God is revealed there and God commands His blessings mysteriously upon the people like morning dew!

The ruling prince and satanic strongmen over a family, territory, community and nation represent a more formidable adversary and require corporate prayers and anointing in UNITY to subdue and take possession of our inheritance. Pastor Yonggi Cho of South Korea's testimonies is a reliable life testimony. He attributes his success in South Korea to the binding up of the strongman over the nation in one accord. He is the founder of the world's largest church of over 800,000 members.

If God's people intend to take the earth for the Kingdom of God, they must first take the heavenlies. The strongman over each area, life and family must be bound in order to release the souls of men, women and children.

These strongmen over a single person, families, territory and nations will not bow to just a single saint. This is the reason God designated His true Church, the body of Christ, to defeat principalities (Jeremiah 51:20-22). That's why Jesus said: "I will build my church and the gates of hell shall not prevail against the church" – Matthew 16:18.

It takes the united effort of God's saints to bind up the strongman over different areas. No individual saint fights this battle alone. One of the assignments of God's end-time army is to do war in the heavens against Satan in unity.

Satan knows there is power in unity, and that is why he tries his best to keep the body of Christ divided. Unity brings an anointing upon the church that Satan cannot stand against (Psalm 133)! Where there is unity, God will command the blessing, "even life forevermore". In the end-times, God's true church will move in a unity the world has never before seen.

There is tremendous anointing that flows when believers in Christ Jesus come together in one accord with one voice, one mind, one love and one common agenda. Jesus Himself demonstrated this on Earth. All through His ministry, He worked together with the Heavenly Father and the Holy Spirit as three in one. He often drew strength from the three-in-one, the trinity.

"Again I say to you that if two of you agree on earth concerning anything that they ask, it will be done for them by My Father in heaven. For where two or three are gathered together in My name, I am there in the midst of them." – Matthew 18:19-20

THE POWER OF UNITY

Unity is the secret of overcoming the lies of the devil and taking possession of our Kingdom inheritance. Unity is a very powerful weapon in the believer's hands that the devil cannot fight against. One ministering angel can destroy thousands of satanic host in a moment.

Remember, where two or three are gathered together in one accord in the name of God, He is there in their midst! Disunity is a weapon of defeat in the hands of the enemy. Satan has been using the spirit and demons of disunity and discord to steal believers' heavenly Kingdom inheritance a long time ago in the Garden of Eden.

"For where two or three gather in My name, there I am with them". – Matthew 18:20 (NIV)

The secret in this scripture is that anywhere God is present; His ministering angels with their flaming swords are also present! This is amazing. Angels that excel in strength are always present in any place where an altar is raised to the Almighty God in unity with one accord. They are often waiting for our command and detailed instructions to carry out God's work for us. It is actually their delegated duty and responsibility. This is why we make them redundant and jobless when we do not realise the fact that they are there to help us and fight territorial battles for us.

"...that all of them may be one, Father, just as You are in me and I am in You. May they also be in us so that the world may believe that You have sent me. I have given them the glory that You gave me, that they may be one as we are one – I in them and You in me – so that they may be brought to complete unity. Then the world will know that You sent me and have loved them even as You have loved me." – John 17:21-23 (NIV)

The glory of God will only be revealed and manifest in the church when the saints of God understand how to work together in unison and with perfect love that cast out all fear. God operates in unison with the Trinity from the foundation of the Earth. He reasons together with the Trinity before He executes His counsels. God does not also work alone; He is not a lone ranger.

UNITY IN THE CORPORATE BODY

When believers in Christ Jesus come together in unity of purpose, there is unlimited anointing that flows in their midst. Unity in the corporate body of Christ edify the body and glorify God. When two or three believers come together in unity, they will be immersed in anointing that flows from each one of them, which draws God's awesome presence mightily and produces supernatural miracles.

"As a prisoner of the Lord, then, I urge you to live a life worthy of the calling you have received. Be completely humble and gentle; be patient, bearing with one another in love. Make every effort to keep the unity of the Spirit, just as you were called to one hope when you were called; one Lord, one faith, one baptism, one God and Father of all, who is over all and through all and in all." – Ephesians 4:1-6 (NIV)

"But to each one of us grace has been given as Christ apportioned it. This is why it says: When He ascended on high, He took many captives and gave gifts to His people. (What does

'He ascended' mean except that He also descended to the lower, earthly regions? He who descended is the very one who ascended higher than all the heavens, in order to fill the whole universe.) So Christ Himself gave the apostles, the prophets, the evangelists, the pastors and teachers, to equip His people for works of service, so that the body of Christ may be built up until we all reach unity in faith and in the knowledge of the Son of God and become mature, attaining to the whole measure of the fullness of Christ." – Ephesians 4:7-13 (NIV)

It is crucial for believers to have the revelation of the calling and the election that is upon their life and harness it to prevail against the gates of Hell. Presently, the gates of Hell are prevailing against the Church of God due to the spirit of disunity that is operating in the body of Christ through strife, evil jealousy, envy, competitive spirit and evil ambition because of lack of knowledge and revelation of the power of resurrection that earned believers access to the keys of the Kingdom.

The attitude of individual believers and the corporate body of Christ Jesus in using the keys of the Kingdom to subdue the gates of Hell and restore the glory of God in these last days is crucial.

Every born again child of God has been granted unlimited grace according to the measure of Christ's gift to manifest God's glory and for the equipping of the saints for the work of ministry, for the edifying of the body of Christ, till we all come to the unity of the faith and of the knowledge of the Son of God to perfect man.

To the intent that now, the manifold wisdom of God might be made known by the Church to the principalities and powers in the heavenly places. This secret was made known to us that Satan has been covering from the beginning.

Before Jesus Christ ascended, He led captivity captive, He removed all obstructions and He destroyed the covering of darkness, the veil which has been used to cover the gentiles in order to steal the glory of God that is our original inheritance in Christ Jesus.

Jesus equipped the Church as corporate body and gave us the keys of the Kingdom with delegated authority and power to use the keys to rule, reign, subdue principalities and lock the gates of Hell so it will not prevail against His church.

The attitude of the corporate body of Christ in the understanding of the manifold wisdom of God is very significant. He manifested this wisdom by coming as the King of Glory to the earth in the flesh as Jesus Christ to reorder the Kingdom and collect the stolen keys, dominion and the glory of His kingdom for us to reign as kings and priests on the planet.

When the corporate body of Jesus Christ comes to the revelation and the understanding of the unity of purpose of the body of Christ, and harnesses the individual gifts together as one body to do the will of God and establish His kingdom on the planet to the glory of His name, the gates of Hell will not be able to prevail against the Church.

Corporate anointing that flows from the united body of Christ cannot be faulted nor defeated by the devil. The corporate anointing gives security, shield and seal upon believers in Christ Jesus. Unity produces unlimited anointing.

Scripture emphasises the power in fellowshipping together in

Hebrews 10:25: "...not giving up meeting together, as some are in the habit of doing, but encouraging one another – and all the more as you see the Day approaching." (NIV)

It is pleasant and good for brethren to be corporately united together as one household of faith without division, hypocrisy and jealousy but in purity and unity of purpose. God will only be present where there is unity of purpose with love without dissimulation.

Supernatural miracles with signs and wonders happens when there is unity in the corporate body of Christ.

UNITY OF PURPOSE IN PRAYERS

"Therefore if you have any encouragement from being united with Christ, if any comfort from His love, if any common sharing in the Spirit, if any tenderness and compassion, then make my joy complete by being like-minded, having the same love, being one in spirit and of one mind. " – Philippians 2:1-2 (NIV)

As believers in Christ Jesus, we have received diverse gifts, which carry different measures of spiritual authority. When we come together in prayers, we honour one another and make room for one another's gifts.

The synergy of our spiritual authority with one accord carries supernatural anointing that moves mountains and destroys the principalities and powers with signs and wonders. Satan dreads believers synergising and coming together in one accord to pray.

We honour God with the power of agreement as we appreciate one another's gifts without jealousy and focusing on one another's differences. We shut the gates against the devil when we determine not to judge or accuse one another but bless and intercede for one another with a pure heart of love.

The last battle will be won through the unity of the body of Christ. It will take unity and love without dissimulation for the body of Christ to take back their Kingdom inheritance and restore the glory of God the Father in families, cities and the nations.

Unity is power.
Unity is an unbroken access.
Unity is an undivided attention.
Unity is a very strong weapon of victory.
Unity is a strong alliance.
Unity is love without hypocrisy.

STRATEGIC OPERATIONAL PRINCIPLES OF THE KEY OF UNITY

- Come together in one accord with believers that are of like passion in unity of purpose. Make sure you are in perfect agreement with one another.

- Repent of any presumptuous sins, unforgiving spirits with bitterness and other personal iniquities. Repent towards one another of any form of resentment whatsoever. Satan often uses the sin of unforgiveness against believers' prayers. That is why most prayers in the Church are hindered!

- Do identification repentance of all the sins and iniquities of the elders and leaders in the Church. This includes political leaders, traditional leaders, kings and queens and the iniquities of the fathers in the families, the territory, land and nations (Leviticus 26:40-42).

- Repent of the sins of locking the Holy Spirit out of the Church and the unholy alliances of the Church with idolatry.

- Acknowledge the sovereignty of God and the Holy Spirit over your life as your Helper, Advocate, Teacher, Comforter and the Revealer of all truth. Confess your weakness and ask the Holy Spirit to come afresh in His fullness upon you and help you!

- Be in perfect agreement with the Trinity and pray in tongues.

- Identify and pull down every stronghold in your life, family, territory, community and nation which the kingdom of darkness is operating from. Destroy the strongholds by holy fire in one accord.

- Send all the strongmen, principalities and powers that are ministering upon the strongholds into everlasting bondage.

- Cut off all their linking cords and command their weapons of war to enter their own heart and their bows to be broken completely (Psalm 37:15 Psalm 144:6).

- At the blast of the breath of God's nostrils command the stars to fight the enemy in their courses and send terrible confusion into their midst and scatter them (2 Samuel 22:14-16).

- Command all the gates to be open and the everlasting doors that have been locked against the souls of people, your inheritance and against the establishment of the Kingdom of God in that domain, territory, family and nation which has hindered the Will of God to be done and made manifest (Psalm 24).

- Command any covering of darkness over the souls of men, women and children and over the nation to be destroyed (Isaiah 25:7-8).

- Command a release in one accord to the souls of the people in the land, nation and release of your Kingdom inheritance.

- Send forth the angels now to go and recover all your inheritances that have been stolen. Declare that you take back your Kingdom inheritance for the fulfilment of the purpose of God in Jesus' powerful name (Hebrews 2:14).

- Seal the victory up with Holy Communion and declare the victory in the name of Jesus, the Lion of the Tribe of Judah.

- Pray as the Holy Spirit directs and instructs you to pray (Romans 8:14).

- Rejoice in the victory! (Revelation 12:11).

There is supernatural breakthrough with profound victory whenever Christians pray in perfect unity with the Trinity. Unity is a mystery. Throughout His ministries, Jesus never worked alone. He was always in perfect agreement with the Father and the Holy Spirit. Disunity is a weapon of defeat in the hands of the ruler of this present world! The devil is defeated when believers offer prayers in perfect unity.

"Two are better than one, because they have a good return for their labour." – Ecclesiastes 4:9 (NIV)

"Though one may be overpowered, two can defend themselves; A cord of three strands is not quickly broken." – Ecclesiastes 4:12 (NIV)

Wherever two or three Christians begin to unite in purpose, there will be a multiplication of power and fruitfulness. The demonstration of unity among Christians will draw unbelievers into the Kingdom of God.

This will release more definition and focus to the Body of Christ than it has had in generations. This is the beginning of what, over the next decade, will eclipse the experiences of the first-century Church.

THE KEY OF KINGDOM LOVE

"Jesus replied: 'Love the Lord your God with all your heart and with all your soul and with all your mind.' This is the first and greatest commandment. And the second is like it: 'Love your neighbour as yourself.' All the Law and the Prophets hang on these two commandments." – Matthew 22:37-40 (NIV)

The new commandment that was given and taught by Jesus Christ Himself about love is quite profound. The first and greatest commandment is to love God with all our heart, soul and mind. This is the first love that every true Christian must first experience on Earth by accepting Jesus as their Lord and Saviour, surrendering all to Him, knowing that He loved us first – even while we were sinners. He came in human flesh and died a shameful death because of the love and compassion He has for us as His creation and the work of His hands.

The second commandment is to love your neighbour as yourself. He said, love your neighbour 'as yourself' – meaning that you have to love yourself first before you can really love your neighbour.

God Himself is love. He first loved you even while you were yet unborn in your father's loins. Everything about God is love. He cannot cease loving us because He created us for His own pleasure and glory. Even while we were yet sinners, He made plans to reconcile us back to Himself by paying the sacrifice of coming to this earth in the flesh and live among us for Him to reconcile us back to His original purpose. Because His name is Love, He cannot stop loving us and having companionship with us.

Our foundational identity is LOVE since we are created in His image of LOVE, we must love as He also love and gave His only begotten Son to die for us. God love for us is indescribable!

"But because of His great love for us, God, who is rich in mercy, made us alive with Christ even when we were dead in transgressions – it is by grace you have been saved." Ephesians 2:4-5 (NIV)

We must identify with the great love that God has for us even before we were born. Right from the foundation of the earth, He loved us for His own pleasure. We must also demonstrate this love first by loving ourselves and identifying with Jesus Christ, His life, His death, resurrection and ascension. Having a strong sense of identity in Him that is called LOVE, then we can demonstrate the love towards our neighbors and other believers who we can see face-to-face. If we do not first love ourselves by identifying with Jesus and His work of redemption, we cannot easily love our neighbors.

"This is how love is made complete among us so that we will have confidence on the Day of Judgment: In this world we are like Jesus. There is no fear in love. But perfect love drives out fear, because fear has to do with punishment. The one who fears is not made perfect in love. We love because He first loved us." – 1 John 4:17 – 19 (NIV)

How wonderful it is to know that we are loved by a mighty God who holds the whole universe in His hands. He does not despise, reject or judge us based on our deeds and character. He loves us more than anyone else on Earth.

"See what great love the Father has lavished on us, that we should be called children of God! The reason the world does not know us is that it did not know Him." – 1 John 3:1 (NIV)

"And hope does not put us to shame, because God's love has been poured out into our heart through the Holy Spirit, who has been given to us." – Romans 5:5 (NIV)

The Holy Spirit pours the love of God into our hearts. The knowledge of God's love transforms us from nobody to somebody, from natural to supernatural. God's love produces hatred for sin and gratitude towards God. His love sanctifies our hearts and produces thirst and hunger for righteousness and truth. Self-worship is banished from our hearts as our hearts are renewed through the love of God.

The love of your neighbour can only spring forth from the love of God. When the love of God spreads in our hearts, our hearts are unified with the Lord and filled with light.

When your heart is full of light without the covering of darkness, you will hear the voice of God clearly, you will know the mind of God, you will see others as God sees them, you will have compassion for lost souls and you will be able to fulfil your kingdom purpose on the planet.

LOVE IS WORSHIP

"Love the Lord your God with all your heart and with all your soul and with all your mind and with all your strength." – Mark 12:30 (NIV)

God is well pleased when you worship Him genuinely with all your heart, your soul, your mind, your strength and all your possessions. God is not interested in halfhearted commitment, partial obedience and partial devotion. When Jesus said: "Love God with all your heart and soul", He was talking about genuine and heartfelt worship. God looks directly into the attitude of your heart as true worship comes directly from the heart.

That is why Jesus told the Samaritan woman that God is Spirit and His worshippers must worship Him in truth and in spirit (John 4:24).

Inasmuch as God created human beings in His own image with spirit, soul and body, the body responds to the soul, the soul responds to and serves the spirit and the spirit responds to and serves God directly. Worship is your spirit responding to God's spirit and that spirit is LOVE. When the love of God spreads in your heart, you will love and serve God deeply with all your soul, spirit and body, which is your worship.

When you share God's love with the unlovable, your neighbour, the poor and the needy, sharing what you have with them is an act of worship to God. Kingdom love goes with sacrifice; it is not always convenient or comfortable but is a commandment to love with all your strength.

God made you in His own image to love you, and he longs for you to love Him back. He created Adam and Eve; He loved them and kept them in a very beautiful and inspiring Garden of Eden. He desired that they love Him as he has loved them and have fellowship with them in the cool of the day.

He longed for their complete obedience as an act of their worship and evidence of their love for Him in return. If you love God, you will obey Him completely, not partially. Partial obedience is an act of disobedience. When you share God's love with an unbeliever and win a soul for Christ, you are worshipping God and showing forth His glory, which is your reasonable service unto God.

You are wonderfully created with unique gifts, talents and potential to manage the earth, to act like Him, reason like Him, think like Him with intellectual capacity and His manifold throne grace to manifest these gifts and dominate the earth. You worship God when you serve others with your gifts and talents.

Since God is a jealous God, He wants all that He created to worship Him without reservation. You will not be able to worship God in truth and in spirit without His love spread over your heart

God's love and kindness shines upon us like the Sun that rises in the sky (Luke 1:78). The level of love that is in your heart is the measure of God that dwells inside of you. Love fulfils the law.

REVELATION OF GOD'S LOVE

God's love towards us is perfect because it is unconditional, non-judgmental, and comes with no strings attached. The Bible says when we were His enemies; He showed His great love for us by sending Christ to die for us.

"But God demonstrates His own love for us in this: While we were still sinners, Christ died for us." – Romans 5:8 (NIV)

It is imperative for you to have a revelation about the love of God as that revelation brings transformation and elevation. When you do not have a revelation of the Father's love for you, as well as what it means to be His sons and daughters, you can easily forfeit the spiritual blessings that God has reserved for you. After all, we are joint heirs with Christ and God wants us to act like Him!

The fact is, God has blessed us with every spiritual blessing. It is your inheritance. You need a revelation of God's love and your Kingdom identity in Christ Jesus, which is your inheritance and the spiritual blessings that God wants you to receive and enjoy. We have been blessed to know, and to be transformed by the exceeding revelatory knowledge of the love of God.

"It was just before the Passover Festival. Jesus knew that the hour had come for him to leave this world and go to the Father. Having loved his own who were in the world, he loved them to the end." – John 13:1 (NIV)

The love of Christ for His own did not stop at the point of His crucifixion. He showed Himself to the disciples after His resurrection, treated, and admonished them most lovingly. That love has continued up to date.

"...just as Christ loved the church and gave Himself up for her to make her holy, cleansing her by the washing with water through the word, and to present her to Himself as a radiant church, without stain or wrinkle or any other blemish, but holy and blameless." – Ephesians 5:25-27 (NIV)

If you are one of those who have placed their faith in Christ and was saved from sin by His grace, you can rest assured that Christ loves you with a special love and that you are fearfully and wonderfully made.

LOVING YOURSELF

In loving yourself after ascertaining your first love for God, you must discover who you are, your Kingdom identity, why you were born and the purpose of your existence on Earth.

It is essential for you to understand the three seasons of human existence on earth; the birth season, discovery/manifestation season and the expiring season.

Your birthday is the season you were born into this Earth, when you will cry out loudly to announce your star and the beginning of your labour on Earth. You will cry out, your parents will be rejoicing and be glad while you cry. The level of your parents' knowledge and revelation will determine the strength of your foundation and your greatness.

The discovery and manifestation season is the season when your parents are supposed to nurture your gifts and the stars in you, prepare, and mentor you to manifest your glory.

The Holy Spirit plays a vital role in helping you to discover your gifts and purpose on the planet. This is why it is crucial to connect with the Lord Jesus Christ as early as possible when you are able to confess your sins and accept Jesus Christ as your personal Lord and Saviour. This will give you the right direction to fulfill your purpose and you will be able to love your neighbour as yourself.

The transition and expiry season is the season of unlimited grace and strength. This is the season during which you have to be as passionate about loving others as God loves you. A season to look for the good in other people and seeking to live a life of love in preparation to exit the earth and face the judgement.

HOW DO I LOVE MYSELF?

- Discover your purpose on the planet.

- Identify with Jesus Christ – the giver of all gifts.

- Appropriate the grace of God upon your life according to the measure of your gifts to fulfill your purpose and manifest your glory.

- Understand the sacrifice that Jesus Christ has paid out of love for you to earn the grace that you have received.

- Understand the fact that you cannot fully utilise the grace and bear fruit without loving other believers and teaming up in unity of purpose.

- Understand the strength and power in unity of purpose with other believers and love without hypocrisy and evil jealousy.

- Understand that true Christ-like love is continuous and unconditional towards all saints without exception.

- Understand that love casts out all fear.

- Understand that where love dwells, God's presence will be.

KINGDOM LOVE

"I in them and You in me – so that they may be brought to complete unity. Then the world will know that You have sent me and have loved them even as You have loved me." – John 17:23 (NIV)

The revelation of the love that God has for the Son the Lord Jesus, is the same love that God showed towards us while we were yet sinners.

This Kingdom love is unconditional love, loving us for who we are and not what we do. If you love God, you will always want to please Him and do His pleasure and His will absolutely in all things. The love of Christ mingled with the love for Christ is the right blend for the true Christian. He is such Lord and Saviour that He is touched with the feeling of our infirmities.

He cares and is powerful enough to walk you through your earthly struggle and take you to heaven at last. Rick Warren said that knowing and loving God is our greatest privilege, and being known and loved is God's greatest pleasure.

STRATEGIC PRAYERS

- Lord, I hereby reject every satanic deposit in my heart and receive the true LOVE of Jesus as replacement.

- Lord, I ask for the power of Christ-like love that betrayal and unfaithfulness of false brethren cannot kill in my heart.

- Give me deeper grace to love unconditionally like Jesus.

- Let there be thirst and renewed grace for "first love" among the brethren in the fellowship (Revelation 2:3-5).

- Love yourself and prioritise the purpose of your existence on Earth. Learn how to harness your gifts and cooperate with other believers to fulfil your eternal Kingdom destiny. Then you will be able to love your neighbour, knowing fully that you are working together to enforce the kingdom of God on Earth and His will absolutely until we come to the full understanding of Ephesians 4:1 - 6:

"As a prisoner for the Lord, then, I urge you to live a life worthy of the calling you have received. Be completely humble and gentle; be patient, bearing with one another in love. Make

every effort to keep the unity of the Spirit, just as you were called to one hope when you were called; one Lord, one faith, one baptism; one God and Father of all, who is over all and through all and in all." (NIV).

CHAPTER 7

THE KEYS OF REPENTANCE AND FORGIVENESS

Repentance is the translation of a Greek word, metanoia that means "turning back" or "return" – a change in our way of thinking.

Repentance is a call to turn from treasuring anything on Earth above God. True and genuine repentance involves the complete turnaround of our mind, thoughts, imaginations and distorted attitudes in a new and righteous direction with new life in Christ Jesus.

Repentance is humility. The Lord gives grace to the humble but the proud He knows afar. Through repentance, we set in place the voice of the blood of Jesus. We can only draw the mercy of God from Heaven when we bring genuine repentance with a humble spirit and a contrite heart.

Our repentance will only be attended to in the courts of Heaven when we humble ourselves without arrogance, pride and self-righteousness but in total surrender.

"Jesus answered, "Do you think that these Galileans were worse sinners than all the other Galileans because they suffered this way? I tell you, no! But unless you repent, you too will all perish." – Luke 13:2-3 (NIV)

"My sacrifice, O God, is a broken spirit; a broken and contrite heart you, God, will not despise." – Psalm 51:17 (NIV)

We draw the attention of the cloud of witnesses in the courts of Heaven upon the Mountain of Zion, through our humility and genuine repentance.

Repentance is a decision to turn away completely with Godly sorrow from dead works, from all the works of the flesh, evil ways, hypocritical attitudes and all unrighteousness.

THE BENEFITS OF REPENTANCE

Genuine repentance changes your identity right from your inner being; it turns your eyes away from yourself to Jesus. It makes you see Jesus at the center of your life. It makes you see beyond the lies of the devil, who tells you that you can continue in sin and iniquities and still be a Christian.

The first thing that happens to someone that truly repented is that the covering of darkness that veiled the heart will be destroyed and the light of God's countenance will penetrate the heart and remove the covering of darkness. As the darkness subsides, the distorted attitude and the filthy garments you have been covered with will be exposed to you in the real sense as sinful habits.

When Jesus died the veil in the temple was turned and there was access for the light to shine from the throne of mercy. Immediately Jesus proclaimed, "It is finished". The temple cloth was ripped in two after He finished the redemptive work of our salvation, deliverance and given us express access to the throne, the holiest of all through His blood.

True repentance gives a new definition to your life as you surrender the old self and distorted ways of life completely to God and yield yourself to Jesus Christ as your personal Lord and Saviour. You become a new creature and a brand new personality.

Genuine repentance brings the baptism of the Holy Spirit upon you, which is the power that works within you and identifies you with Christ Jesus. The manifestation of the gifts of the Holy Spirit with the evidence of speaking with new tongues confirm your true repentance and change in your distorted attitude. Your attitude is the way you perceive things and think. It often exercises a profound influence upon the way you live your daily life and respond towards the flesh and other people in life.

A genuine repentant soul will want to obey the law of the Spirit and disobey the illegal law of the flesh. It is the Spirit who gives life; the flesh profits nothing (John 6:33).

True repentance gives you the benefits of the Kingdom. However, as many as received Him, to them He gave the right to become children of God, to those who believe in His name.

To believe means to entrust yourself to the crucified and risen Jesus. It means to identify with Him as God who came in human flesh, lived among men without sin, suffered at the hands of men and bore the pain and the agony of death for our redemption. God resurrected Him from death and He has come to make His abode in as many that love Him and believe in His words and keep his commandments.

"If you love Me, keep My commands. And I will ask the Father, and He will give you another advocate to help you and be with you forever." – John 14:15-17 (NIV)

True and genuine repentance empowers you with the Kingdom keys, makes you an heir of the Kingdom and entitles you to all the benefits of the heirs of the Kingdom. It gives you access to the delegated authority of believers in Christ Jesus to dominate the earth and live an abundant life in Christ Jesus.

Genuine repentance should firstly be personal. Confession of your personal transgressions, iniquities, and presumptuous sins in your motives, thoughts, imaginations and every unrighteous act must be confessed with your mouth genuinely before you can communicate with God at the throne of grace and have the attention of the heavenly hosts.

Repentance gives God access to intervene and open the doors of favour and mercy.

"Who may ascend the mountain of the Lord? Who may stand in His holy place? The one who has clean hands and a pure heart, who does not trust in an idol or swear by a false god." – Psalm 24:3-4 (NIV).

IDENTIFICATIONAL REPENTANCE

"Those of you who are left will waste away in the lands of their enemies because of their sins; also because of their ancestors' sins they will waste away. But if they will confess their sins and the sins of their ancestors – their unfaithfulness and their hostility toward me, which made me hostile toward them so that I sent them into the land of their enemies – then when their uncircumcised hearts are humbled and they pay for their sin, I will remember my covenant with Jacob and my covenant with Isaac and my covenant with Abraham, and I will remember the land." – Leviticus 26:39-42 (NIV)

The iniquities of the ancestors and in the bloodline go as far as the fourth generation if it has not been confessed and atonement is not made through the blood of Jesus.

The majority of the issues we battle with, which cause the gates of Heaven to close above us whenever we go to the altar of prayer, are the consequences of our ancestral sins and iniquities that have not been atoned for or brought to the place of repentance at Calvary for cleansing. The devil is careful to use the unconfessed ancestral iniquities, written codes and law of sins and unrighteousness against us and hinder our prayers.

Although we have not committed the sins and iniquities, we came from the bloodline, the root of the tree that bore the fruit from that lineage. We need to do identification repentance, by identifying with the sins as the Holy Spirit reveals it to us and bring genuine repentance through the blood of Jesus for cleansing and forgiveness.

If we are interceding for the Church, thrones and nations, we should first identify with the sins of the leadership in the church, political leaders and traditional leaders and ask God to forgive all errors, idolatry and shedding of innocent blood the land, corruption, nepotism, homosexuality and all other iniquities.

However, true and genuine repentance is never a once off experience. Repentance should be a way of life and a lifelong process; inasmuch as we are still living in the flesh we are bound to be ensnared by the weight of sins and iniquities, which easily beset us. This is why we must make repentance our way of life with humility from our spirit man.

FORGIVENESS

"Therefore each of you must put off falsehood and speak truthfully to your neighbour, for we are all members of one body." – Ephesians 4:32 (NIV)

"Forgive us our sins, for we also forgive everyone who sins against us. And lead us not into temptation." – Luke 11:4 (NIV)

Forgiveness is divine. The Greek word translated as "forgive" in the New Testament, aphiemi, means to remit (a debt), to leave (something or someone) alone, to allow (an action).

Forgiveness is key to restoration, joy and peace in the Holy Spirit and it goes with righteousness, love and purity in your heart.

You cannot forgive easily and let go if you do not carry the love of God genuinely in your heart. If you want to enjoy the peace of God in your heart with the Joy of the Lord in the fullness of the Holy Spirit, which is actually the Kingdom of God, you have to learn how to forgive easily.

Forgiveness is vital to your emotional health and spiritual survival. Unforgiveness leads to a stronghold of bitterness and ill health. No wonder, in the letter written to the Jewish believers in Hebrews it was stated clearly that believers must pursue peace.

"Make every effort to live in peace with everyone and to be holy; without holiness no one will see the Lord. See to it that no one falls short of the grace of God and that no bitter root grows up to cause trouble and defile many." – Hebrews 12:14-15 (NIV)

Unforgiveness and bitterness is one of the weapons the accuser of the brethren, the devil, uses against believer. It is a poison to the soul.

Forgiveness liberates the heart from bondage and cleanses the mind from all impurities and toxins. Any believer in Christ Jesus who refuses to forgive does not have peace in the soul nor communion with God.

"This is how my heavenly Father will treat each of you unless you forgive your brother or sister from your heart." – Matthew 18:35 (NIV)

If you can forgive easily, forget and move forward, then the LOVE of God is shed abroad (spread) in your heart. If you desire to know how much of God is in you, check your love for others and how easily you forgive.

- Unforgiveness is sepsis (serious illness) of the soul. It puts your heart into captivity and bondage.

- Unforgiveness forms a stronghold of bitterness in your heart.

- Unforgiveness blocks the heavens above you and hinders your prayers.

- Unforgiveness withdraws your peace. There is no peace for the wicked.

- Unforgiveness delays your blessings.

- Unforgiveness makes you vulnerable to satanic attack and opens the gates of your life and family to snares and pestilence.

Your relationship with others is dented by unforgiveness. Unforgiveness is the quickest method of killing a generation. Whatever your haunting memory is, you must begin to declare your deliverance from its bondage.

"It (love) does not dishonor others, it is not self-seeking, it is not easily angered, it keeps no record of wrongs." – 1 Corinthians 13:5 (NIV)

People will do or say things that offend you. Forgive them and do not hold grudges. Having an unforgiving heart leads to bitterness and a heart that is bitter cannot love, as it ought to love. When you cannot love, you become carnally minded. A carnally minded person cannot please God.

Peter asked Jesus: "Lord, how often will my brother sin against me, and I forgive him? As many as seven times?" Jesus said to him, "I do not say to you seven times, but, seventy-times seven."

Forgive every day without counting how many times you have been wronged. Forgiveness is not an option but a virtue to be lived by every true Christian. Blessed are you if you forgive, because in turn your father in Heaven will forgive you.

Unforgiveness is a transgression of the law and ordinances of the Kingdom, which could be used against you by the accuser of the brethren in any way.

"Settle matters quickly with your adversary who is taking you to court. Do it while you are still together on the way, or your adversary may hand you over to the judge, and the judge may

hand you over to the officer, and you may be thrown into prison." – Matthew 5:25 (NIV)

For us to agree with our adversary quickly means we quickly forgive and release the person immediately without keeping record of the past wounds. The root of bitterness is a very dangerous issue that we should be very careful and diligent to shake off from our hearts. Unforgiveness leads to the root of bitterness, which later forms a stronghold and a throne of iniquity in our hearts with the ruling strongmen!

The Lord taught me personally that the reason why we have to forgive easily and let go most often is so that our prayers and sacrifices will not be rejected before the throne of grace in the court of Heaven.

However, repentance and forgiveness should never be a once off believers' experience, but rather a way of life and a lifelong process. As long as we still live in the flesh, we are bound to be ensnared by the weight of sins and iniquities, which easily beset us. This is the reason we must make repentance and forgiveness our way of life as David often practiced.

David often cried to God for the purging of his heart, as we are saved by the grace of our Lord Jesus Christ, not by the works of our righteousness nor our strength.

THE UNPARDONABLE SIN – BLASPHEMY AGAINST THE HOLY SPIRIT

Jesus Christ was given to us to shed His blood and die a shameful death on the cross, for us to have the forgiveness of our sins and be reconciled to God.

There is only one sin in the whole of the Bible that is an unpardonable sin, which is blasphemy against the Holy Spirit of God.

"Anyone who speaks a word against the Son of Man will be forgiven, but anyone who speaks against the Holy Spirit will not be forgiven, either in his age or in the age to come." – Matthew 12:32 (NIV)

This scripture indicates that blasphemy against the Holy Spirit is an eternal sin, which is sin against God Himself. The Holy Spirit personifies the power of God. Blasphemy against the Holy Spirit is a final rejection of God's grace. Jesus Christ is the wisdom and the grace of God given for our redemption from the bondage of sin and iniquities. The continual rejection of Jesus Christ, with an unrepentant heart is blasphemy against the Holy Spirit.

Blasphemy against the Holy Spirit, specific as it was to the Pharisees' situation in the Bible, cannot be duplicated today. Jesus Christ is not on Earth and no one can personally see

Jesus perform a miracle and then attribute that power to Satan instead of the Holy Spirit.

The unpardonable sin today is that of continued unbelief in the death and resurrection of the Lord Jesus. There is no pardon for a person who dies rejecting Jesus Christ and His redemptive purpose on Earth.

The Holy Spirit is at work in the world today, convicting the unsaved of sin, righteousness and judgement. If anyone resists the conviction of the Holy Spirit, and remains unrepentant, then he is choosing eternal damnation, Hell over Heaven.

"But very truly I tell you, it is for your good that I am going away. Unless I go away, the Advocate will not come to you; but if I go, I will send Him to you. When He comes, He will prove the world to be in the wrong about sin and righteousness and judgment: about sin, because people do not believe in Me; about righteousness, because I am going to the Father, where you can see Me no longer; and about judgment, because the price of this world now stands condemned." – John 16:7-11 (NIV)

Without faith, it is impossible to please God, and the object of faith is Jesus Christ. There is no forgiveness for someone who dies without accepting Jesus as his Lord and savior by faith and through the Holy Spirit. God has provided for our salvation in His Son. Forgiveness is found exclusively through the shedding of the blood of Jesus. To reject Jesus, the only Saviour, is to be left with no means of salvation and to reject the only pardon is, obviously, unpardonable.

STRATEGIC OPERATIONAL PRINCIPLES – REPENTANCE AND FORGIVENESS

- Repentance is a key to open the Throne gates of Heaven.

- Identify all sins, iniquities, unrighteousness and wickedness at personal level as you approach the Throne of grace upon your altar of prayers.

- Acknowledge that you have indeed sinned against God and that you have done wickedness against your creator.

- Confession is very important; confess all your known sins in words, actions, deeds and evil imaginations.

- Ask the Lord for forgiveness and cleansing by the blood of Jesus.

- Confess all accusations by the accuser of the brethren in any way the devil may be accusing you of anything known and unknown.
- Identify all the family sins and iniquities; confess the sins, for instance in Africa, all our ancestors have worshipped idols and things that God created, animals, stones, river goddesses and the likes. They have practiced Freemasonry, witchcraft and sorcery. That is rebellion against the God of Heaven.

- All these abominations must be confessed diligently with deep repentance before God.

- Atonement must also be made by the blood of Jesus to cleanse all the sins and iniquities for God to show His mercy and forgive.

FORGIVENESS

Forgiveness is a top priority in the Kingdom of God. Jesus regarded it as a top priority in the Lord's Prayer. He expects His children to forgive one another, just as God forgives us. If you fail to forgive, you are violating the Kingdom order and thereby playing into Satan's hands.

When Jesus teaches us to pray that God would forgive us, "for we ourselves forgive," he is not saying that the first move in forgiveness was our move. Rather, it goes like this: God forgave us when we believed in Christ (Acts 10:43). Then, from this broken, joyful, grateful, hopeful experience of being forgiven, we offer forgiveness to others.

A forgiving spirit signifies that we have been saved and our sins are forgiven. When we forgive others, it shows that we have faith and that we are united to Christ. We are indwelt by the gracious, humbling Holy Spirit.

When God forgives after repentance, He also forgets completely. God wipes away our sins and iniquities through the blood of Jesus after genuine repentance and he would not remember them again.

- Acknowledge the significance of the cross. It is the cross of Christ that makes forgiveness legally and morally right.

- Make a decision in your heart to forgive anyone who offends and hurts you for any reason.

- Mention the name of the person that have hurt you and confess that you forgive him/her.

- Draw the blood of Jesus upon your heart to cleanse your heart from all forms of bitterness and hurt.

- Pray for the person to also find the freedom of forgiveness and come out of the bondage into the glorious liberty of the Son of God. Bitterness is a serious bondage!

- Give thanks to God for the spirit of grace that brings refreshment and restoration after confession and forgiveness.

PRAYER

O Lord, wash away from me by the blood of Jesus every hurting memory of past hurts, offences and abuses, as I release the offenders, in Jesus' powerful name. I forgive myself in any way I have hurt anyone in Jesus' powerful name.
I receive grace from the Throne of mercy to forgive always in Jesus' powerful name. Amen.

CHAPTER 8

THE KEY OF THE BLOOD OF JESUS

"Then I heard a loud voice in heaven say: 'Now have come the salvation and the power and the kingdom of our God, and the authority of His Messiah. For the accuser of our brothers and sisters, who accuses them before our God day and night, has been hurled down. They triumphed over him by the blood of the Lamb and by the word of their testimony; they did not love their lives so much as to shrink from death.'" – Revelation 12:10-11 (NIV)

The blood of Jesus is a powerful key and strong weapon that silences the voice of the devil, the accuser of the brethren. Satan and his host hates to hear that Jesus died and rose again. After Jesus Christ ascended up on high, He presented the blood at the throne of God in the courts of Heaven, thereby preventing Satan and his cohorts from reaching the third Heaven, because the blood cries daily at the throne of God. The testimony of the blood of Jesus is very powerful before God's throne. The blood speaks!

The disturbing question that Satan does not have an answer for is the shedding of the blood. God shows mercy based on the voice of the blood of Jesus, the blood of the everlasting covenant.

Verdicts are often given in the courts of Heaven, based on the testimony of the blood of Jesus. The voice of the blood of Jesus is the strongest voice that testifies in the courts of Heaven, which is often raised as a standard against every accusation from Satan and his cohorts in heavenly places and on the earth beneath.

The blood of the everlasting covenant has the ability to release the verdicts as it is written in the scroll concerning the Church, the nations and us. The blood of Jesus is a very powerful weapon that has a voice that does not stop crying out for judgement and mercy. There is fire and life that speaks in the blood of Jesus.

The accusations of the accuser do not have any power against the brethren, inasmuch as the brethren can appropriate the blood to answer for all accusations with the word of their testimony.

THE KEY ELEMENTS IN THE BLOOD OF JESUS

Three major key elements operate effectively inside the blood of Jesus: the voice, the fire and the light that are contained in the blood of Jesus.

THE VOICE OF THE BLOOD

The voice of the blood of Jesus is very powerful because it is the Blood of the righteous, the blood of the one who knew no sin. By the wisdom of God, He had to come into the world in the flesh and live a sinless life among men for Him to be qualify to take the scroll, lose the seven seals and re-order the Kingdom, execute judgement and take back with power and authority all that Satan has stolen from the Garden of Eden.

The voice of the blood of Jesus often cries out on behalf of the brethren for vengeance, justice and mercy. It cries out profusely and testifies in favour of what it was shed for, in other words to enforce the verdict on Earth and cry for vengeance over the adversaries.

The voice of the blood of Jesus disarms the sting of death and the host of darkness. It releases the humility of the Lamb of God. The voice of the blood of Jesus destroys the strongholds of the grave; it destroys fear, despair, strife and frustration and brings peace, love and unity.

The voice of the blood of Jesus breaks bondage and destroys the power of darkness, witchcraft manipulation and bewitchment and it speaks liberation and restoration to people's lives.

"But you have come to Mount Zion, to the city of the living God, the heavenly Jerusalem. You have come to thousands upon thousands of angels in joyful assembly, to the church of the firstborn, whose names are written in heaven. You have come to God, the Judge of all, to the spirits of the righteous made perfect, to Jesus the mediator of a new covenant, and to the sprinkled blood that speaks a better word than the blood of Abel." – Hebrews 12:22-24 (NIV)

"They triumphed over him by the blood of the Lamb and by the word of their testimony; they did not love their lives so much as to shrink from death." –Revelation 12:11 (NIV)

When you appropriate the blood of Jesus and use it by faith genuinely by the leading of the Holy Spirit, the blood speaks deliverance, healing, miracles, redemption, freedom from bondages and restoration.

Jesus' death and resurrection established His Kingdom and dominion over the kingdom of darkness. Jesus' death and resurrection is our glory as believers in Christ Jesus.

The shedding of His blood and His resurrection makes Christianity unique and makes it stand out from all other religions in the world. The leaders of all other religions died and were buried; only Jesus rose from the grave because the grave could not hold on to Him. He is alive forevermore. Jesus' blood is powerful, is real and still applicable today as

He heals, saves and delivers from death and the power of the grave.

The voice of the blood of Jesus speaks protection from the snares of the evil one. The voice of the blood of Jesus is full of power and majesty that the devil cannot resist. Satan has no answer for the evidence of the blood of Jesus.

The voice of the blood of Jesus is a very powerful weapon to rule, reign, subdue and silence the voice from the grave and dominate our Kingdom inheritance on Earth.

MY ENCOUNTER WITH THE POWER IN THE BLOOD OF JESUS

I heard the voice of the Lord audibly in my room three times, as He gave me instruction to go to a specific hospital. I questioned the voice twice when He asked me: "Where is your brother?" I answered: "My brother is at the church." I heard the voice the second time and I answered the same, but when I heard the same question the third time, I was convinced that God was busy with a task He wanted me to carry out.

I asked the Lord, "Where is my brother?" He said: "Your brother is in Eko Hospital", and I was shocked. To prove the voice right, I went to Eko Hospital.

As l was approaching the hospital, l saw my brother's car in front of the hospital and l went inside the male medical ward and saw my brother in very deep agony and pain.

He told me that l should quickly call the doctor for him because he could not breathe well. I rushed to call the doctor, but l was shocked to see the doctor and the nurses not even perturbed. Little did l know that they have given up on my brother the previous night as they had given him all the best treatment, but they knew that he would not survive.

I was standing outside the room on the doctor's instruction when one of the hospital cleaners told me that my brother was calling me. As l entered, my brother held my hand and said to me, "Janet, l have to die. Tell our parents not to be sorrowful because I have made peace with God and I will see Jesus and I am going to make it to Heaven". He continued, "Check my inner suit pocket, access my bank account and do whatever you like with the money in my account ..." As he was speaking, he suddenly dropped his hands and died. This was the first time I ever saw a person die.

I immediately set up an altar and a throne there beside his bed, and started interceding. I connected the throne to the throne of God and continued to bring my strong reasons why my brother must not die at that point and why God had to let him live to fulfil his eternal Kingdom purpose and finish his race.

I interceded for almost thirty minutes before I heard the first instruction audibly again: "Cast out the spirit of death". I obeyed immediately and as I cast out the spirit of death, I heard another instruction; "Hold one of his veins and pass the Blood of Jesus through his vein". I quickly knelt down, held his left hand and looked for one of his veins, held it up and passed the blood of Jesus through the vein.

I did this the first time, and immediately the hand that was dead cold started getting warmer. As I passed the blood the second time, it was as if electric power passed through the hand. After the third time, his entire body became very warm as life came back to the body through the blood of Jesus.

Suddenly, he took his hands from me and opened his eyes wide with a new countenance and vibrant eyes completely different from the agonized eyes that I had met on that bed before he died. When God restores, it is total restoration!

My brother was raised from death through the power of the blood of Jesus, the resurrection and life. He was discharged the same day. All the nurses and doctors and the other patients in the male medical ward were astonished. I went home with my brother the same day.

Since then my brother has become a full-time preacher of the gospel of the Kingdom of Jesus; The resurrection and life raised him from death with perfect healing.

The full account of these powerful testimonies of the power in the blood of Jesus, and how my older brother was raised from death, his experience and life after being dead for 30 minutes, are written in another book.

When we identify with Jesus' suffering, pain, the sacrifice of His blood, His death, burial and resurrection, we become a new creation, we have a brand new identity to rule and reign with Him.

Jesus' cross, His birth, death and resurrection changed your identity on the planet. His death and resurrection gives you a secured identity. The cross is the highest altar, the hallmark of mercy.

The cross-changed our identity from an ordinary personality to a divine and supernatural entity.

The cross makes you untouchable to the power of darkness because you bear the mark of the Lord Jesus upon your body.

Jesus' blood as a main key of the Kingdom was used to possess the gates of darkness and caused the devil to hand over the keys of Hell and death to Jesus.

Jesus handed the keys over to believers with authority and power to subdue the kingdom of darkness and dominate the earth to the glory of our God.

The voice that speaks from the Blood of Jesus is the voice of the Lord. The voice of the Lord is powerful and filled with majesty. It breaks the cedars of Lebanon. The voice of the Lord divided the flames of fire.

"The voice of the Lord strikes with flashes of lightning. The voice of the Lord shakes the desert. The voice of the Lord twists the oaks and strips the forests bare. And in His temple all cry, 'Glory!'" – Psalm 29:7-9 (NIV)

The testimony of the voice of the blood of Jesus speaks powerfully at the throne of grace. Jesus' blood cries out for our forgiveness and redemption at the throne of grace in the court of Heaven. When the accuser of the brethren approaches to accuse the believers at the courts of Heaven, the voice of the blood of Jesus cries out for mercy for the saints of God.

The sacrifice of the blood of Jesus purchased and reconciled all of creation back to God, the Creator of all things. The blood of Jesus often cries out for mercy, and grants God the legal right as judge to dominate the earth on our behalf.

Jesus' blood will keep crying out for the redemption of all creation and nations before the Throne of God, until the Kingdom of God is established in the heart of every person that God has created and His will is done on Earth, as it is in Heaven.

The Church of God that was purchased and redeemed by the blood must agree with the testimony of the blood of Jesus. Believers are the stewards of Jesus' sacrifice on Earth. We must agree with the testimony of the blood of Jesus, as the blood serves as legal testimony on our behalf in the courts of Heaven at the Throne of God.

The Blood of Jesus proclaims a powerful testimony with which we must perfectly agree to subdue the kingdom of darkness and to establish the Kingdom of God on Earth.

THE FIRE IN THE BLOOD

There is fire in the blood of Jesus that purifies and restores. During my first year at university, I had an ardent Muslim as my roommate.

As an ardent Christian, I often had my quiet time during the early hours of the day. When my Muslim roommate discovered this, she made sure to wake up early to do her incantation on the mat inside the same room where I have raised an altar to the God of Heaven.

I was always angry and felt very uneasy whenever she was doing her Muslim prayers. I discussed the burning issue with God quietly, and the Lord gave me an instruction. He said to me, lay a siege for her with the blood of Jesus and send her out of the room.

I asked God how I lay a siege. The Lord instructed me to pour the blood of Jesus in the four corners of the room and release the fire in the blood to burn every strange spirit in the room. I prayed over a small bottle of olive oil and drew the blood of Jesus inside the bottle. I poured the blood at the entrance and in the four corners of the room.

After lectures, I came back to the room before her. When she came back, I saw that she felt uneasy. She suddenly started to pack all her belongings and moved out of the room the same day and until I graduated from the university, I never lay my eyes on her again. I learned about the fire in the blood of Jesus on that day.

The story of my brother's resurrection from death taught me about the real fire that burns in the blood of Jesus. Before I had heard the instruction from the Lord to cast out the spirit of death and pass the blood of Jesus into his veins, his hands and legs were deathly cold. As I passed the blood of Jesus the first time and second time, I began to feel the fire flowing up from his legs to his hands and the third time; he took his hands from me and opened his eyes with a new countenance and a completely restored body.

His body also received strength as the blood of Jesus flowed into his body. There is supernatural strength and power in the blood of Jesus that gives total restoration and supernatural healing.

THE LIGHT IN THE BLOOD

The blood of Jesus is full of powerful light that dispels darkness. That is why the grave could not hold Jesus. The hosts of darkness cannot operate where there is light; it is illegal for darkness to operate where there is light.

The light that shines in the blood of Jesus like the sun in its strength destroyed the thick darkness inside the grave and the grave was unable to hold Jesus. The light of the blood of Jesus broke the grave.

Jesus destroyed Satan's hierarchical set-up inside the grave by the light of His blood. The host of darkness cannot stand the full light that shines through the blood of Jesus. He led captivity captive when He entered the grave and the full light that shines through the blood destroyed the host of darkness.

The blood of Jesus is a powerful key of the Kingdom that Jesus used to prevail against the gates of Hell and death!

JESUS SHED HIS BLOOD IN FIVE PLACES

The five places on the body of Jesus where His blood was shed forms a strong spiritual significance for our victorious living on Earth and our Kingdom dominion as believers in Jesus Christ.

THE HEAD

The head governs all bodily functions, controls the five senses and serves as the control panel for your body. Jesus wore a crown of thorns on our behalf and through it earned the victor's crown for us. We can take up this crown by taking all our thoughts captive and bringing them into obedience of God's will. He restored the crown of thorns for crown of glory though His blood. He restored our king-Priest identity to rule, reign, subdue principalities and dominate the Earth to His glory! He restored our Spiritual Antennae with light and perfection to walk in wisdom, intuitive understanding, insights, inspiration, knowledge and counsels from the mind of Christ.

The blood that He shed with pain from His head, restore our perspectives to life, He restore our wrong mind set and mediocrity with lack of knowledge, so we will no longer perish but dominate the Earth to the glory of His name.

THE TWO HANDS

Jesus suffered wounds in His two hands when they were nailed to the cross. The pain He bore and the blood that He shed gave us skilful hands to do His good deeds and be creative restorers through His blood. Through the blood that came out of His hands, restore the work of our hands and makes whatever we lay our hands upon to prosper. He shed the blood from His hands to restore the productivity and fruitfulness of the works of our hands.

THE SIDE

Jesus' side was pierced and the blood gushed out of His side, which signifies the strength and supernatural power and might that was purchased through His blood. He earned for us the life that begets life. The blood that He shed from His side, restore our strength, power, purity and truth.

THE FEET

Jesus paid the price for us to possess the land as our inheritance and to dominate the earth with the blood that He shed from His feet in preparation for us to go out into the world and claim His territory wherever our feet touch the ground. The blood restores our straight walk with God, not conforming to the world, but perfect conformity with the image of God.

"I will give you every place where you set your foot, as I promised Moses. Your territory will extend from the desert to Lebanon, and from the great river, the Euphrates – all the Hittite country – to the Mediterranean Sea in the west. No one will be able to stand against you all the days of your life. As I was with Moses, so I will be with you; I will never leave you nor forsake you." – Joshua 1:3-5 (NIV)

JESUS PRESENTED HIS BLOOD IN FIVE PLACES

THE FIRST HEAVEN (LAND)

Jesus has redeemed the earth by shedding His blood and has therefore earned the right for us to dominate the earth through His blood. We have to take up that authority and speak life over the territory that was stolen at the Garden of Eden.

Jesus Christ redeemed the land with His blood of the everlasting covenant and His blood restored all things. This is the reason why Satan does not have a legal claim over the land and its fullness.

The earth is our inheritance with all its fullness. All the false altars that Satan has raised through idolatry and evil covenants are illegal. Once a well-informed believer in Christ Jesus uses the delegated authority to destroy the evil altars and send all the ministering demons of the altar into captivity, the evil altar becomes powerless. Then the Blood of Jesus will raise a new altar in its place.

"The earth is the Lord's and everything in it; for He founded it on the seas and established it on the waters." – Psalm 24:1-2 (NIV)

THE GRAVE

Jesus Christ presented His blood inside the grave as an evidence of victory and a weapon to disarm the host of darkness inside the grave. He took back our Kingdom dominion and the keys of the Kingdom through the sacrifice of His blood. As He presented His blood at the grave, Satan and his host were defeated. Satan had to release the keys of the Kingdom to our inheritance by the blood.

"When the perishable has been clothed with the imperishable and the mortal with immortality, then the saying that is

written will come true: Death has been swallowed up in victory. Where, O death, is your victory? Where, O death, is your sting? The sting of death is sin, and the power of sin is the law." – 1 Corinthians 15:54-56

DOUBTING THOMAS

The blood of Jesus was presented to doubting Thomas Didymus who refused to believe until he could see and feel the wounds inflicted upon Jesus on the cross.

"Now Thomas (also known as Didymus), one of the Twelve, was not with the disciples when Jesus came. So the other disciples told him, "We have seen the Lord! But he said to them, "Unless I see the nail marks in His hands and put my finger where the nails were, and put my hand into His side, I will not believe." A week later his disciples were in the house again, and Thomas was with them. Though the doors were locked, Jesus came and stood among them and said, "Peace be with you!" Then He said to Thomas, "Put your finger here; see my hands. Reach out your hand and put it into my side. Stop doubting and believe." Thomas said to Him, "My Lord and my God!" John 20:24-28 (NIV).

We must overcome the devil by the blood of the Lamb and by the confession of our faith testimony.

THE THIRD HEAVEN

The blood of Jesus was presented at the throne of God where the twenty-four elders are casting down their golden crowns and worshipping God with the innumerable company of angels and the four living creatures.

The blood of Jesus is at the center of the throne of God, crying for mercy for the saints of God to this day! The reason why Satan cannot get to the third heaven is because the blood of Jesus is there as a true witness against the accusations of Satan against the saints.

"Jesus said, 'Do not hold on to me, for I have not yet ascended to the Father. Go instead to my brothers and tell them, I am ascending to my Father and your Father, to my God and your God'" – John 20:17 (NIV)

THE BLOOD AS A SEAL OF THE NEW COVENANT

"Now may the God of peace, who through the blood of the eternal covenant brought back from the dead our Lord Jesus, that great Shepherd of the sheep, equip you with everything good for doing His will, and may He work in us what is pleasing to Him, through Jesus Christ, to whom be glory forever and ever. Amen." – Hebrews 13:20-21 (NIV)

The everlasting covenant is the covenant of grace made with Jesus Christ when you accept Him as your Lord and Saviour. With this covenant, you enter into a contractual relationship, a legal covenant that is binding between you and Jesus with terms and conditions. The covenant is sealed with His blood and lasts forever.

God will always keep the promise of His covenant with you. Your responsibility in fulfilling the terms and conditions of the everlasting covenant is to obey all His commandments and to worship only God.

Worshipping God in truth and in spirit is the most important aspect of the covenant. God deals with human beings on a covenant basis. No man will be in close relationship with God without a Kingdom covenant relationship. God even dealt with David, the man after His own heart, only through a covenant. He made a covenant with His anointed and beloved children.

When you accept Jesus Christ as your personal Lord and savior, you enter into an everlasting covenant relationship, surrendering your will and your life to God in acknowledgement of His death, His pain and the blood he shed on the cross of Calvary for our redemption. We renew this everlasting covenant when we share Holy Communion as a church family.

After conversion, we yield ourselves to Him in obedience to His will as part of the terms and conditions of the everlasting covenant and He fulfills His part based on the terms of the everlasting covenant, which He has sealed with His blood. This covenant brings us peace, prosperity, protection, healing, cleansing, redemption and victory.

THE BLOOD AS A SEAL OF PROTECTION

The blood of Jesus serves as a security guard and seal of protection when you imprint it upon your forehead, upon the entrance of your door and the gates of your heart.

"The blood will be a sign for you on the houses where you are, and when I see the blood, I will pass over you. No destructive plague will touch you when I strike Egypt." – Exodus 12:13 (NIV)

The blood of Jesus has power to protect us from the evil power of the enemy. It was the blood of the Lamb, sprinkled on the doorposts of their houses, which protected the children of Israel in Egypt. God said: "When I see the blood, I will pass over you".

The blood of Jesus has power to save you and your entire household if you believe and abide by the terms and conditions of the covenant. All the benefits of the covenant will be transferred unto you without reservation forever and God will never break His covenant.

THE BLOOD CLEANSES

It is only by the blood of Jesus that our hearts can be cleansed from all sin and unrighteousness. If we say we have no sin, we deceive ourselves and the truth is not in us. If we confess our sins, God is faithful and just to forgive us our sins and to cleanse us from all unrighteousness through the Blood of Jesus Christ.

Jesus purchased us for God by His blood of the everlasting covenant from every tribe, language, people, and nation to make us priests to serve God.

"If we confess our sins, He is faithful and just and will forgive us our sins and purify us from all unrighteousness." – 1 John 1:9 (NIV).

THE BLOOD HEALS

The blood of Jesus has power to heal and restore. It heals all afflictions and illness in the body, soul and spirit. When the blood of Jesus is sprinkled upon the area of affliction in your body, it heals and restores your health to the original state.

"Surely He took up our pain and bore our suffering, yet we considered him punished by God, stricken by Him, and afflicted." – Isaiah 53:4-5 (NIV).

THE POWER OF THE BLOOD IN HOLY COMMUNION

Taking Holy Communion has restorative power. That is why Paul recommend the act of partaking in Holy Communion as a church in unity, as a powerful weapon against the accuser of the brethren.

"For I received from the Lord what I also passed on to you: The Lord Jesus, on the night He was betrayed, took bread, He broke it and said, 'This is My body, which is for you; do this in remembrance of Me.' In the same way, after supper he took the cup, saying, 'This cup is the new covenant in my blood ; do this, whenever you drink it, in remembrance of me." – 1 Corinthians 11:23-25 (NIV)

When you partake of the body and blood of the Lord Jesus in unity of heart and purpose, you identify with the pain, agony and sacrificial death of Jesus on the cross of Calvary. You are declaring the death and the resurrection of the Lord Jesus.

The secret and weapon of victory in Holy Communion, is that Satan hates to hear that Jesus died and shed His blood for us. Satan does not want you to declare that Jesus died and rose from death. Satan hates being reminded that he had to surrender the keys of life and death to Jesus and that Jesus has given us the authority to have dominion on Earth.

"For whenever you eat this bread and drink this cup, you proclaim the Lord's death until He comes." – 1 Corinthians 11:26 (NIV)

As often as you proclaim the death and resurrection of the Lord Jesus, you are affirming the defeat of Satan over your inheritance. You are claiming your legal right to your healing and deliverance from every form of evil affliction.

"Then I heard a loud voice in heaven say: 'Now have come the salvation and the power and the kingdom of our God, and the authority of his Messiah. For the accuser of our brothers and sisters, who accuses them before our God day and night, has been hurled down. They triumphed over him by the blood of the Lamb and by the word of their testimony; they didn't love their lives so much as to shrink from death." – Revelation 12:10-11 (NIV)

Partaking in the Lord's Supper, His blood and body by faith, shows that we are remembering Jesus Christ's sacrifice for us and renewing our pledge of service and commitment to

Him. Satan does not have an answer for the blood of the new covenant, which seals our Kingdom covenant relationship with God. Through the ordinance of the Holy Communion, we are qualified to prevail over all the storms of life, win every battle and overcome because Jesus overcame after paying the full price by His blood of the everlasting covenant.

Taking the ordinance unworthily portrays ignorance of the implications of Christ's sacrifice at Calvary. How then do we partake in the Lord's Supper? We must do so carefully and thoughtfully, with humility, contrition of heart, honour and due reverence to God. That way we receive the full blessing and Kingdom benefits of the holy sacrament.

The Lord's Supper is intended not only to commemorate the supreme sacrifice at Calvary, but also to enable us to spiritually incorporate into ourselves the very life and essence of the death of Jesus. This will enable us to live for Him.

Through it, believers are reminded of the death of the Saviour and of the hope and imminence of His return. Sadly, the Corinthian church soon lost its true meaning and replaced it with wanton discrimination between the rich and the poor. Paul promptly cautioned them and presented to the church the significance and process of conducting the Lord's Supper, as given by the Lord.

The Lord's Supper is a supernatural weapon of war.

STRATEGIC OPERATIONAL PRINCIPLES

- Acknowledge the sacrifice of Jesus' shameful death on the cross and the pain He bore through the shedding of His blood.

- Appreciate the gifts of the Blood of Jesus and the power that the blood carries.

- On a daily basis, draw the blood of Jesus from the throne of grace at the court of Heaven and sprinkle the blood upon every gate that leads to your heart.

- Sprinkle the blood of Jesus upon the gates of your mouth and ears, for whatever you care to listen to and look at will have a direct effect upon your heart.

THE BLOOD OF JESUS FOR SUPERNATURAL HEALING

- Draw the blood of Jesus from the throne of grace and pass the blood through your veins by faith.

- Sprinkle the blood on the afflicted area in your body by faith.

- Pass the blood through your navel for healing and restoration.

- Sprinkle the blood of Jesus at every gate that has been opened through ancestral practices and use the blood to shut all the gates.

- Sprinkle the blood of Jesus on every part of your body where you got incisions or tattoos.

- Sprinkle the blood of Jesus on your food before you cook it and before you eat.

- Take Holy Communion often in remembrance of the death and resurrection of the Lord Jesus. There is supernatural healing and refreshing that comes from your inner man when you partake of the flesh and the blood of Jesus in obedience to the ordinance.

CHAPTER 9

THE KEY OF THE HOLY SPIRIT

"But you will receive power when the Holy Spirit comes on you; and you will be my witnesses in Jerusalem and in all Judea and Samaria, and to the ends of the earth." – Acts 1:8 (NIV)

The Holy Spirit is the spirit of truth and the only divine personality that knows the truth about you. The gift of the Holy Spirit is the seal of our salvation. He is the one that gives us the assurance that we are born again.

The Holy Spirit is the oxygen in our blood and the evidence of God dwelling within us. Without the presence and the power of the Holy Spirit manifesting in us, we are just like any other unbeliever in the world.

The blood of Jesus that He shed on the cross of Calvary makes a significant difference between Christianity and any other religion. He is the personality living in us and revealing the truth in the Word to us, He is the Spirit of Truth, whatever He hears from God the Father is exactly what He will reveal and make known to us.

"If you love me, keep my commands. And I will ask the Father, and He will give you another advocate to help you and be with you forever – the Spirit of truth. The world cannot accept Him, because it neither sees Him nor knows Him. But you know Him, for He lives with you and will be in you. I will not leave you as orphans; I will come to you." – John 14:15-18 (NIV)

These last days are the days of the Holy Spirit. We are in the millennium of the Holy Spirit. The Holy Spirit is God living inside of us as the power that actually works within us.

The Holy Spirit has been poured upon us because Jesus has been glorified. The Holy Spirit is the grace of God in us. The Holy Spirit sustains us in sickness and all forms of afflictions.

When the Holy Spirit came upon Mary, she conceived supernaturally without knowing a man. Jesus fulfilled His ministries, He broke the power of the grave, He conquered death by the power and help of the Holy Spirit.

The Holy Spirit regenerates believers; He interprets the Bible and edifies the word of God. He gives boldness with divine audacity and confidence not to be intimidated by anyone in any category, but to rule over the kingdoms of the earth and inherit the nations by the power of the Holy Spirit. The Holy Spirit is the scepter and power of the kingdom of God and is the scepter of righteousness and holiness.

Salvation precedes the gift and baptism of the Holy Spirit. Without confession of our sins, there is no remission of sins. After salvation, before the Holy Spirit could come upon us with the evidence of speaking with new tongues, we must be sure we keep all His commandments and be sure that we harbor no secret sins in our hearts.

The Holy Spirit may not fully manifest with an evidence of speaking with new tongues if there is no genuine repentance with sanctification. He is the Spirit of truth and He is absolutely holy. He understands what goes on in the depths of your heart.

The Holy Spirit will not manifest until you keep God's commandment with a pure heart. Although He is in us, He will not manifest in an unholy vessel. He is a holy personality, God in us, living in us and revealed through us. He is God's muscles and power inside of us.

"But the Advocate, the Holy Spirit, whom the Father will send in my name, will teach you all things and will remind you of everything I have said to you." – John 14:26 (NIV)

Oftentimes we fight life's battles alone with the weapons of our flesh, of which the scriptures say it profits nothing. We must rather yield to the Holy Spirit completely and be in perfect agreement with Him to guide, counsel and reveal the truth to us in every situation. He is our helper in all circumstances; He is the person that enables us to pray with the right counsel. Unless we ask anything in His Name according to His will, God may not listen to our prayers.

Most of the time we pray amiss because we have not received counsel from the Holy Spirit, the Spirit of Truth.

The Holy Spirit is the greatest evangelist. Jesus Christ instructed His disciples in Acts 1:4-8: "On one occasion, while He was eating with them, He gave them this command: 'Do not leave Jerusalem, but wait for the gift my Father promised, which you have heard me speak about. For John baptised with water, but in a few days you will be baptised with the Holy Spirit. Then they gathered around Him and asked Him, 'Lord, are You at this time going to restore the kingdom to Israel?' He said to them: 'It is not for you to know the times or dates the Father has set by His own authority. But you will receive power when the Holy Spirit comes on you; and you will be my witnesses in Jerusalem, and in all Judea and Samaria, and to the ends of the earth.'" (NIV)

We must be baptised with the fullness of the Holy Spirit before we can do the will of God. The Holy Spirit is the driving force that will actually work in us to do His will and His good pleasure.

THE HOLY SPIRIT TRANSFORMS

Only those who are filled with the Holy Spirit will transform the world that is covered with thick darkness. The release of the wave of the Holy Spirit will bring global revival to the churches, families and the nations. When our worship is filled with the Holy Spirit, there will be revival.

The Holy Spirit will convict and reproof the world of sin. He will bring great help to us. He also heals our infirmities and weaknesses.

The Holy Spirit transforms our character. He makes true disciples of us because He is interested in maturing our character more than in bringing us personal comfort.

The Holy Spirit leads and gives direction at every point of decision in our life. He will glorify God in us. He empowers us for service and guides us into all truth. He reveals unto us the understanding of our Kingdom inheritance and delivers us from great deception in the last days.

The global reawakening that is coming will be championed by the world changers who will be empowered by the fullness of the Holy Spirit.

We must utilise the power of the Holy Spirit to win the war inside and outside to restore our Kingdom inheritance and take back our nations and kingdoms from the ruler of this present world by fire. The Kingdom comes by power because the devil will never let go or give up!

The keys of the Holy Spirit have been given unto us to win the battle of our Kingdom inheritance. The Holy Spirit has the ability to release your hidden potential. The Holy Spirit is active in us and living inside of us.

We need to understand this perfectly well and use these keys to reign, rule, subdue, dominate and possess all our Kingdom benefits in full. Jesus said: "Because I go to my Father, greater work than I did, you will do. If I do not go, the Holy Spirit of promise will not come. When the Holy Spirit comes, He will teach you all things. Greater works you will do because I go to my Father."

The level of the fullness of the Holy Spirit in you will determine the measure of the grace of God that will be released unto you. The Holy Spirit releases grace. The Holy Spirit releases the measure of grace we need daily to operate our potentials and the gifts of God in us to actualize and fulfil His Kingdom purpose.

The power of the Holy Spirit transforms you from an ordinary person to a divine supernatural personality.

THE HOLY SPIRIT REVEALS JESUS

The Holy Spirit reveals Jesus as a living reality and brings us into a deeper relationship with Him in an ongoing way. Jesus introduces us to the Father, saying;

"...I Am the way and the truth and the Life. No one comes to the Father except through Me." – John 14:6 (NIV).

Jesus reveals the Father, and the Holy Spirit reveals Jesus. It is an interdependent cycle, and we are privileged to participate in it. The Holy Spirit reveals the unified counsel of the Father and the Son. He (the Spirit) does not talk about Himself, He talks about God the Father and Jesus. He listens to their conversations and He speaks about what He hears, on their initiative, not on His own.

He is our life-giving source, the One who brings us into the life of the Lord Jesus. He makes true disciples of us because He is interested in maturing our character more than in bringing us personal comfort. He brings us truth, not false assurance or consolation.

THE HOLY SPIRIT CONVICTS

He convicts, persuades, shepherds, and leads us to the life-source of God. He helps us overcome our fears and He stretches us beyond ourselves, moving us to testify of the love and power of God and showing us how to bear fruit that lasts. We can get to know Him, because He lives inside us. We can lean into Him, walk with Him, live with Him, and listen to Him. We can depend on Him to always lead us out of darkness and into the light.

DO NOT GRIEVE THE HOLY SPIRIT

The Holy Spirit is not only God, but also He has a will, a personality, and He can even be offended!

The Bible specifically warns about desisting from grieving the Holy Spirit, because He is a personality and He can be grieved!

"Do not let any unwholesome talk come out of your mouths, but only what is helpful for building others up according to their needs, that it may benefit those who listen. And do not grieve the Holy Spirit of God, with whom you were sealed for the day of redemption. Get rid of all bitterness, rage and anger, brawling and slander, along with every word of malice. Be kind and compassionate to one another, forgiving each other, just as in Christ God forgave you." – Ephesians 4:29-32 (NIV)

To grieve means to make sad or sorrowful. It means to cause sorrow, pain, or distress. The apostle Paul writes: "Don't use foul or abusive language. Let everything you say be good and helpful, so that your words will be an encouragement to those who hear them. Moreover, do not grieve God's Holy Spirit by the way you live. Get rid of all bitterness, rage, anger, harsh words, and slander, as well as all types of malicious behaviour. Instead, be kind to each other, tender-hearted, forgiving one another, just as God through Christ has forgiven you."

THE SIX SINS THAT MAKE THE HOLY SPIRIT SAD

- Abusive and foul language
- Bitterness and a resentful spirit
- Unforgiveness
- Uncontrolled anger
- Malicious behaviour
- Malice and wrath

STRATEGIC OPERATIONAL PRINCIPLES – HOW TO RESPOND TO THE HOLY SPIRIT

1. *HONOR HIM*: Welcome Him into your own spirit. Acknowledge His companionship and presence inside of you. Acknowledge Him as the third person of the Godhead, with His own distinct personality and ways. As

John the Beloved wrote:

"But when He, the Spirit of truth, comes, He will guide you into all the truth. He will not speak on His own; He will glorify Me because it is from Me that He will receive what He will make known to you." – John 16:13 (NIV)

2.   SEEK HIS PRESENCE. Holy Spirit is our equipper. As we ask for Him, we must seek to be equipped by Him continually so that we can do the work of ministry. He is utterly generous with the gift of Himself, but He wants to be asked.

Jesus put it this way:

"So I say to you: Ask and it will be given to you; seek and you will find; knock and the door will be opened to you. For everyone who asks receives; the one who seeks finds; and to the one who knocks, the door will be opened. Which of you fathers, if your son asks you for a fish, will give him a snake instead? Or if he asks for an egg will give him a scorpion? If you then, though you are evil, know how to give good gifts to your children, how much more will your Father in heaven give the Holy Spirit to those who ask Him!" – Luke 11:9-13 (NIV)

The Holy Spirit will always give us what we ask according to God's will and timing. He will never give us too little or too much. We can never get too full of Him because He increases our capacity along the way.

3. *GIVE HIM LIBERTY.* Once you have welcomed Him into your innermost being, let Him take charge of you. When you allow Him to have full control, you will find true freedom and liberty. You will discover that the Spirit enables you to control the deeds of your human nature. He will transform you completely to the personality that God created you to be on Earth!

4. *ALWAYS PURSUE CONVERSATIONS WITH HIM.* Speak in tongues for at least one hour in the early hours of every day and before you sleep at night. He will begin to reveal secrets and deep things to you.

5. *ASK HIM QUESTIONS.* Most of the time, The Holy Spirit expects us to make inquiry from Him of things we do not understand! Whenever you have dreams, and you do not have the clear picture of the interpretation, ask the Holy Spirit to please tell you the meaning of the dreams.

6. *ASK HIM FOR COUNSEL.* The Holy Spirit is the great counselor the Lord has given to us, to give us counsel, to bring all what He has told us to our remembrance. To be effective is by counsel. Ask the Holy Spirit to give you His counsel concerning any matter you might not understand. He will give you the right direction to make the right choice.

7. *MAKE HIM YOUR CONFIDANT.* The Holy Spirit is well pleased when He knows you have made Him your confidant and best friend. This means, there is nothing you will not be able to discuss with Him in confidence with truth and integrity of heart.

"Now the Lord is the Spirit, and where the Spirit of the Lord is, there is freedom. And we all, who with unveiled faces contemplate the Lord's glory, are being transformed into His image with ever-increasing glory, which comes from the Lord, who is the Spirit." – 2 Corinthians 3:17-18 (NIV)

PROPHETIC MINISTRY OF THE HOLY SPIRIT

In these last days, those who are filled with the Holy Spirit will transform the world. New firebrand believers will be raised and filled with the Holy Spirit for global revival of the youth, women, families, churches, thrones and the nations.

The true worshippers will be empowered by the Holy Spirit to restore the glory of God's kingdom and cover the earth with God's glory as the waters cover the earth. Haggai 2:9-12

There will be a global reawakening that will cause the world transformers to arise by the power of the Holy Spirit and manifest the glory of God among the nations.

The Holy Spirit will reproof the world of sin and unrighteousness.

The Holy Spirit will release manifold grace to do the will of God on Earth as it is being done in Heaven.

STRATEGIC PRAYERS

- Appreciate and acknowledge the sacrifice that Jesus has paid for us by shedding His blood and giving us the gift of the Holy Spirit.

- Acknowledge the gifts of the Holy Spirit and honour the holy presence of the Holy Spirit as your helper, teacher, advocate, and wisdom, revealer of all truth, counsellor and comforter.

- Confess to Him your weaknesses and that without Him you can do nothing because you do not have the power of your own but you are relying absolutely on Him to help you.

- Ask the Holy Spirit to come in His fullness with His new fire upon you and reveal Himself with His light and perfection.

- Ask the Holy Spirit to sharpen your spiritual antennae and polish you like a new instrument in His hand and flood your heart with His light and glory.

- Listen to His prompting and the still small voice. Act immediately on whatever the Holy Spirit speaks to your heart.

- Pray in tongues every day as the Holy Spirit gives utterance and listen to the gentle voice of the Holy Spirit as the Spirit of Truth.

CHAPTER 10

THE KEYS OF THE WORD OF GOD

"For the word of God is alive and active. Sharper than any double-edged sword, it penetrates even to dividing soul and spirit, joints and marrow; it judges the thoughts and attitudes of the heart." – Hebrews 4:12 (NIV)

"The precepts of the Lord are right, giving joy to the heart. The commands of the Lord are radiant, giving light to the eyes." – Psalm 19:8 (NIV)

The word of God is the truth about God and His word is Himself, our shield and buckler, it protects and shields us as we seek to understand His word, lay hold on it and believe Him.

The keys of the word and the voice of God are powerful weapons from the beginning and to the end of the earth. These keys are in twofold; the spoken word and the written word. The word of the Lord and His commandments are pure, the word of the Lord enlightens the eyes and takes away darkness. It is only when there is no light that darkness exists. The word of the Lord is the light that shines onto a perfect day. The light shines in darkness and darkness cannot comprehend it.

"In the beginning was the Word, and the Word was with God, and the Word was God. He was with God in the beginning. Through Him all things were made; without Him nothing was made that has been made. In Him was life, and that life was the light of all mankind. The light shines in the darkness, and the darkness has not overcome it." – John 1:1-5 (NIV)

"The Word became flesh and made His dwelling among us. We have seen His glory, the glory of the one and only Son, who came from the Father, full of grace and truth." – John 1:14 (NIV)

The word of God has power to secure our hope in Him, in inheriting our Kingdom inheritance. The word of God shines forth the light of God, which dispels darkness at all levels.

THE WORD OF GOD OPERATES AT FIVE LEVELS:

- The word of God creates as it is spoken by faith

- The word of God reveals the deep things through the light that shines forth from the word

- The word of God uncovers the darkness over the substance in our life

- The word of God discerns the intent of the heart of every man and reveals the truth

- The word of God performs actions according to God's counsel. Job 12:22

"He reveals the deep things of the darkness and brings utter darkness into the light." – Job 12:22 (NIV)

Whenever you declare the word of God in faith, the Lord watches over His word to perform it. He cherishes His words above His name.

THE KEYS OF THE WORD AND VOICE OF GOD

- The word of God is the heavenly law. The Law of the Lord is perfect, converting the soul.

- The word of God is His strength; the strength of God is inside His word. The word has the strength to take hold of situations, circumstances, and make all things respond to divine order according to God's will.

- The word of the Lord is a perfect law of liberty, setting free the oppressed, giving freedom to the souls of men and turning the hearts of kings towards God.

- As the scripture says: "The law of the Lord is the perfect, converting the soul, the testimony of the Lord is sure, making wise the simple; the statutes of the Lord are right, rejoicing the heart; the commandment of the Lord is pure, enlightening the eyes." (Psalm 19:8)

- The word of the Lord has the ability to take hold of the heart of the king because it is a perfect law of liberty when quoted in truth and by faith.

- The testimony of the word of the Lord has the power to give wisdom to the simple. The word of the Lord and His commandments are pure, it takes away foolishness and gives clear vision with deep insight into the mind of Christ.

The spoken word of God has power to take hold of all that God has created by His word, both living and non-living things. God created all things by His word and called things into existence through the spoken word and this is the reason why the word of God has power to take hold of situations and circumstances when you speak it out affirming it with faith.

The word of God has power to renew the mind and take hold of the heart of man, the thoughts, imaginations and feelings. The word is sharper than any two-edge sword and it pierces through the heart and cuts between soul and spirit, between joint and marrow. It exposes the innermost thoughts and desires of the heart of man.

The word of God is a sword of freedom, it holds the power to uncover darkness in the heart of man and free the heart from old mindsets. It liberates the soul from wrong beliefs and deception, which are the lies of the devil. Lies and deception bring imprisonment and bondage.

The word of God has the ability to convert the soul after liberating it from the bondage of deception and lies of the devil. It has the power to destroy the covering of darkness that supervises deception and enlightening the eyes with the truth of God's word.

The word of God has power to purify the heart and make it viable to rejoice and worship God in truth and spirit. The word of God gives life and creates.
"In Him was life, and the life was the light of men. And the light shines in the darkness, and the darkness did not comprehend it".

The word of God is life and truth, God entered into His word and used the word because the word was with Him from the beginning and the word was Himself.

The word of God carries power and it works wonders when it is spoken by faith. Little wonder why the darkness cannot comprehend and stand the word of God because it carries light, life and truth.

After God formed man of the dust of the ground, He breathed into his nostrils the breath of life, and man became a living being. God's breath and the life that is in Him caused man to become a living being. The living being means a body that God inhabits.

"Then the Lord formed a man from the dust of the ground and breathed into his nostrils the breath of life, and the man became a living being." – Genesis 2:7 (NIV)

Inasmuch as we have the same breath from God the Father and He is the word, we have the transferred authority and power to use the word as God used the word to create and generate light. We need this revelation and the understanding of the power of the word that works inside of us to dominate the earth and its fullness. God gave man this power and the authority to continue to use the word, which is the life that works in us the same way he used the word because He has replicated Himself inside of us.

The understanding of the power of the breath of God inside of us, and the power that we carry in our tongue will give us the boldness and confidence to declare the word of God upon every situation and circumstance to dominate and manage God's creation as designed and planned by God Himself. We also need the revelation that, without the word nothing in Creation would exist. This is the reason why the word of God has the ability to take hold of all things, change situations and re-create.

"Through Him all things were made; without Him nothing was made that has been made." – John 1:3 (NIV)

"The tongue has the power of life and death, and those who love it will eat its fruit." – Proverbs 18:21 (NIV)

Through the breath of God that was breathed into man's nostrils, man's tongue becomes powerful and carries life and death. No wonder Satan used the word to deceive Eve with the covering of darkness and the word took hold of Eve's heart.

Jesus also used the power of the spoken word to defeat the devil in the wilderness of temptation after fasting for 40 days and forty nights. The devil also understands the power of the spoken word and will use it against us.

"The tempter came to Him and said, 'If you are the Son of God, tell these stones to become bread.' Jesus answered, "It is written: 'Man shall not live on bread alone, but on every word that comes from the mouth of God.'" – Matthew 4:3-4 (NIV)

God in His infinite wisdom came in human form through a woman to restore His original purpose for creating man. God needs to accomplish His original purpose for creating man in His own image. He breathed His own breath into the nostrils of man in order to bring man to the position where He will be able to relate, dialogue and fellowship with man for His own pleasure and glory.

His original plan and purpose was that man would also be the managing director of all that He has created. He made man to rule, reign, subdue principalities and powers and dominate the kingdom of the world for His glory.

The word of God is an instrument of praise and worship to glorify God. It is a two-edge sword in our hands to quench all the fiery darts of the enemy and execute vengeance on the nations. He wants all that He has created to always praise His name with His words and speak of all his wonders both in Heaven and on Earth without any other creation sharing His glory.

"All your works praise you, Lord; your faithful people extol you. They tell of the glory of Your kingdom and speak of Your might,

so that all people may know of Your mighty acts and the glorious splendour of Your kingdom. Your kingdom is an everlasting kingdom, and Your dominion endures through all generations." – Psalm 145:10-13 (NIV)

Understand that the life of God is in your mouth and the fire of the Holy Spirit ignites your tongue to release resurrection power to cast down arguments, pull down strongholds and bring every thought into captivity in obedience of Christ.

"The weapons we fight are not the weapons of the world. On the contrary, they have divine power to demolish strongholds. We demolish arguments and every pretension that sets itself up against the knowledge of God, and we take captive every thought to make it obedient to Christ. And we will be ready to punish every act of disobedience, once your obedience is complete." – 2 Corinthians 10:4-6 (NIV)

Through the word of God, you can change situations, transform your life, circumstances and people around you.

The word of God enhances spiritual growth. Spiritual growth is the process of replacing lies with truth. Jesus prayed earnestly: "Sanctify them by the truth; your word is truth." Sanctification requires revelation. The revelation of the truth of the word of God sanctifies believers in Christ Jesus and shapes us to fulfill God's kingdom purpose and finish strong.

The word of God gives live abundantly, God's word generates life, brings comfort, overcomes adversity, brings things into existence, frightens the devil, purifies the heart, brings joy, defeats temptation and transforms circumstances

THE VOICE OF GOD

The voice of God is powerful and is full of majesty. The devil cannot stand the voice of the Lord. When God speaks, the word carries power and it will never come back without performing God's counsel.

"The voice of the Lord is over the waters; The God of glory thunders; the Lord thunders over the mighty waters. The voice of the Lord is powerful; the voice of the Lord is majestic. The voice of the Lord breaks the cedars; the Lord breaks in pieces the cedars of Lebanon. He makes Lebanon leap like a calf, Sirion like a young wild ox. The voice of the Lord strikes with flashes of lightning. The voice of the Lord shakes the desert; the Lord shakes the Desert of Kadesh. The voice of the Lord twists the oaks and strips the forests bare. And in His temple al cry, "Glory!" The Lord sits enthroned over the flood; the Lord is enthroned as King forever. The Lord gives strength to His people; the Lord blesses His people with peace." – Psalm 29:3-11 (NIV)

The throne is a place of authority, a place of decree and command. The throne is a place where judgements are pronounced, a place of manifesting the glory and power of God. The voice of God is the operational instrument upon the thrones.

STRATEGIC OPERATIONAL PRINCIPLES

- Believe the word of God

- You cannot effectively use what you do not believe. You have to believe that the word of God is everything (2 Corinthians 1:20).

- Martin Luther remarked: "I make my Amen strong and I know that God is surely listening to me, I do not make room for doubt". Refuse to doubt the word of God. It is the belief in the word of God that gives light, not mere listening to the word. If you do not believe the word of God, it cannot produce enough force to propel a shift in your life.

- Accept the authority of the word. Believe that the word of God is full of majesty (Psalm 29).

- Believe that God magnified His word above all His name (Psalm 138:2)

- Believe that the word of God gives power and strength

- Believe that the word of God uproots strongholds (2 Corinthians 10: 4-6)

- Apply the principles of the word of God into all situations, problems and circumstances.

- Pray the word of God. Praying God's word is the most powerful and effective prayer believer in Christ Jesus can offer for a victorious living. It is imperative to learn to pray the prophetic promise of the word back to God.
  "The effectual fervent prayers of a righteous man availeth much." – James 5:16

To unlock the prophetic promises of God during every season in your life, you need to pray the promises of God in His word over your life.

There are three ways you can use the word of God to pray effectively:

- Proclamation
- Declaration
- Thanksgiving

The word "proclaim" is derived from a Latin word, which means "to shout fort" or "to shout aloud". The word significantly means to declare something with boldness and strength. The devil does not have an answer against the true word of God because there is nothing he can do against the truth but for the truth. This is the reason the declaration of the true word of God is a very powerful weapon against the devil.

David declared the word of the Lord against Goliath with boldness and confidence, and the word of the Lord took hold of Goliath and killed him. It was the declaration of the true word of God that actually killed Goliath before the stone hit his forehead. There is power in the spoken word of God.

PRAISE AND WORSHIP THROUGH GOD'S WORD

"Let the faithful people rejoice in this honour and sing for joy on their beds. May the praise of God be in their mouths and a double-edged sword in their hands; to inflict vengeance on the nations and punishment on the peoples." – Psalm 146:5-7 (NIV)

"In God, whose word I praise, in the Lord, whose word I praise – ..." – Psalm 56:10 (NIV)

While they were in jail, at midnight Paul and Silas were praying and singing hymns to God, and the prisoners were listening to them. Suddenly there was a great earthquake so that the foundations of the prison were shaken; and immediately all the doors were opened and everyone's chains were loosed.

Praises and worship are weapons of warfare, praising the word of God is a powerful weapon of victory. God sits enthroned on the praises of His people.

Praises will transform your feelings and worship will open God's throne room. God created us to worship Him and praise Him in the beauty of His holiness.

When we praise Him with His words, he delights in us because we are fulfilling His original heart's desire for creating man in His likeness – so He can have a creature that will praise Him and worship Him with his words for His glory and pleasure.

Paul and Silas praised and worshiped God in prison with the word of God as the two-edged sword in their hands. The sword is in your hand and the fire of the Holy Spirit is upon you and the sword. Arise with the high praises of God in your mouth and the sword of the word of God in your hand to pull down the strongholds of darkness that has exalted itself against the truth and life of Christ in you.

"I will bow down toward Your holy temple and will praise your name for your unfailing love and your faithfulness, for you have so exalted your solemn decree that it surpasses your fame." – Psalm 138:2 (NIV)

Jesus earned the authority for us to be in charge, manage creation and dominate the earth. Jesus spoke directly to His disciples and said to them anything they allow on Earth will be allowed in Heaven and anything they disallowed with the word of their mouth, shall be disallowed in Heaven.

It is very clear here that it is not God who forbids or allow things on Earth but rather His disciples, those who are called by His Name, who are born again and filled with the Holy Spirit. We give God permission to act on Earth through the word of our prayers and prophetic declaration.

Therefore, you and I control what happens on the earth through what we allow and what we forbid. We allow things to happen on Earth primarily by the words we speak and through our prophetic declaration.

If we always speak negative things over our life, children, home, territory and Nations we are in fact opening the gates and allowing evil spirits that cause these things to operate in our lives and in all ramifications.

HEARING GOD'S VOICE

God created the earth through the spoken word. He also sent Jesus, His only begotten Son as the word that lived among us. God still speaks to those who believe in Him and accept Jesus as their personal Lord and Saviour.

As believers in Christ Jesus, it is imperative to discover and understand how God speaks and relates to you. Hearing God's voice requires you to train your spiritual senses and be filled with the Holy Spirit. You need to be familiar with the language of the Holy Spirit and have an intimate relationship with the Holy Spirit and often living in God's presence.

"But Samuel was ministering before the Lord – a boy wearing a linen ephod." – 1 Samuel 2:18 (NIV)

Samuel learned to live in God's presence, he learned to LISTEN and RESPOND to God. As a consecrated reigning priest, Samuel was always properly dressed with his consecrated priestly attire – a linen ephod which symbolised purity inside and outside – with the fullness of the Holy Spirit. He separated himself from all the appearances of darkness that cover the earth; he purified his heart with all diligence and did not allow his garments to be polluted.

He consecrated his ears, not having itching ears that listen to gossip and unproductive conversation that impair the spiritual ears from hearing God's Voice clearly. Samuel understood that he was into a covenant Relationship with God and he determined to be a useful vessel in God's hand and a blessing to his generation.

"The Lord was with Samuel as he grew up, and He let none of Samuel's words fall to the ground. And all Israel from Dan to Beersheba recognised that Samuel was attested as a prophet of the Lord. The Lord continued to appear at Shiloh, and there he revealed himself to Samuel through his word." – 1 Samuel 3:19-21 (NIV)

Samuel grew up under Eli's tutelage, but God bypassed Eli and started speaking to Samuel after Eli lost his credibility before God. Eli lost his kingdom focus; he blinded himself to his error, failure, assumptions and presumptuous sins.

Although Eli was always present in God's tabernacle, he was always distracted and full of unproductive activities. Suddenly there was a paradigm shift in his motives, thoughts, imagination, attitude, devotion, preferences and perspectives to life and the word of God.

Eli could no longer discern, see clearly and hear God's voice for his generational redemptive purpose. No wonder Eli turned to folly with secret faults and presumptuous sins with his two sons. Eli could no longer see and discern the abomination that was standing right in the holy tabernacle of God. What is a priest doing in God's tabernacle if he can no longer hear the voice of God clearly?

To this day God is still busy revealing deep secrets to those who fear Him and dwell in His awesome presence in this deceptive world, and particularly in this defining season that we are for us to be able to be His true representatives and fulfil God's redemptive purpose. We must listen to His voice carefully.

STRATEGIC PRAYERS

- Lord, show me your mercy and cleanse me from all secret faults that may prevent me from hearing you clearly.

- Lord, keep me back from presumptuous sins that may block my spiritual inner ears from hearing your voice.

- Lord, deliver me from a flat nose and marred vision that cannot discern and let your fire consume every defect in my eyes that l may see clear visions.

- Lord, deliver my mind from distractions while l am in your presence that l may be focused and hear you clearly by the power of the HOLY SPIRIT.

- Lord, my heavenly Father, consume by FIRE the spirit of error and the abominations standing in the churches globally, that your GLORY may dwell in our Land and Nations.

"But whoever listens to Me will live in safety and be at ease, without fear or harm." – Proverbs 1:33 (NIV)

Presently, lots of distractions, deception and noises are preventing us from listening, hearing and responding to God's voice. Yet the heavens are declaring the glory of God daily, day unto day uttered speech and night unto night reveals His deep knowledge!

However, how many people are listening and responding? It is time to move from the realm of mere activities and move to the realm of revealing and manifesting the Glory of God in our generation, communities and Nation! (Isaiah 60:1-3).

God blessed Samuel with many gifts; he heard clearly from God, he wisely knew what to do in crisis because he could use the keys of the word and voice of God effectively. Little wonder that everyone listened to him. Samuel exuded integrity and honesty with a pure heart. He honestly faced the truth about each area of his life from his FOUNDATION!

He always heard from the mouth of God. Little wonder everyone depended on him to intercede for them and tell them what is in the heart of God!

To this day God is constant. He has a message and is busy looking for a messenger with a consecrated heart that will carry His redemptive purpose and finish it on earth!

Consecration involves revelation about the state of our heart, our motives, thoughts, objectives and intentions in life. True revelation about yourself is all about your HEART.

Who you are in the sight of God is the reflection about your HEART, which is more important to God than what we do for God! When Isaiah's heart and tongue were cleansed, his pattern of vision and revelation changed! (Isaiah 6:1)

STRATEGIC PRAYERS

- Lord my heavenly Father, anoint me afresh with your revelational gifts and knowledge to enable me hear your VOICE clearly and see with clear VISION.

- Lord my God, let the fire of the Holy Spirit consume all things that represent "Ashtoreths" in my life from my foundation that impair my hearing ability and "Uzzaiahs" that blocks my Vision in Jesus name!

- Lord my God, make me a polished shaft and keep me in your quiver, dish me out in due season to manifest Your power and glory!

- The secret things belong to the Lord our God, but those things that He revealed belongs to our children and us forever (Deuteronomy 29:29).

In the past three decades since I have accepted Jesus as my Lord and my Saviour, I have encountered many believers from different walks of life who share a deep desire to hear clearly from God. God takes great delight in revealing His mind to the true believer who worships Him in truth and in Spirit.

OPERATIONAL STRATEGIES FOR HEARING GOD'S VOICE

- Guard your heart with all diligence (Proverbs 4:23).

- Raise a new and true altar to God with a heart of gratitude and consistent worship (Genesis 12:7-8)

- Forgive easily and let go.

- Avoid evil jealousy and competition; you are unique in your calling and purpose. Cast down all arguments and every high thing that exalts itself against the knowledge of God from your heart (2 Corinthians 10:5).

- Bring every evil thought and imagination into captivity to the obedience of Christ.

- Avoid thoughts of bitterness and resentment.

- Do not occupy your heart with unnecessary worries and comments that are irrelevant to your Kingdom purpose.

- Avoid unproductive conversations, gossip, backstabbing and unnecessary jesting. It impairs the ears!

- Put away a deceitful mouth and perverse lips.

- Avoid distraction and but pay attention to the Holy Spirit's prompting in your heart.

- Owe no man anything but love!

- Focus the lens of your heart to God at the throne of grace.

STRATEGIC PRAYERS

- Lord, I acknowledge Your sovereignty over my life, I honor you because of who You are! Thank You for Your word.

- Lord, enlighten my eyes, give unto me an eye salve to see clearly the vision of your kingdom through Your word.

- Lord, enlighten the eyes of my heart to be able to use the word appropriately and effectively.

- Quicken my understanding to know the depth of your strength in your word.

- Lord, ignite the fire of Your word in my heart and shut it up in my bones like a burning fire.

CHAPTER 11

THE KEY OF A PURE HEART

The heart of man is like a battlefield where the battle for dominion is taking place daily. This makes it imperative to guard jealously and keep the heart with all diligence, because all the issues of life flow from your heart.

"My son, pay attention to what I say; turn your ear to My words. Do not let them out of your sight, keep them within your heart; for they are life to those who find them and health to one's body." – Proverbs 4:20-23 (NIV)

The heart of man is very significant in the fulfilment of God's Kingdom mandate. The heart speaks aloud to God more than the mouth and any other organ or part of the body. Food does not defile a man, but all that proceeds from the heart is what defiles a man.

"I will sprinkle clean water on you, and you will be clean; I will cleanse you from all your impurities and from all your idols. I will give you a new heart and put a new spirit in you; I will remove from you your heart of stone and give you a heart of flesh. And I will put my Spirit in you and move you to follow my

decrees and be careful to keep my laws." – Ezekiel 36:25-27 (NIV)

The Lord weighs and tries hearts. God deals directly with the heart of every man He has created. The state of your heart will determine the level of God's grace you will be able to access at the time of need.

The heart of man is a gate to the throne of God. You will not be able to connect with the Throne of God without a pure heart. Little wonder, why Jesus said in the Beatitude, that only those who have a pure heart will be able to see God and access the benefits of His Kingdom.

"Blessed are the pure in heart, for they will see God" – Matthew 5:8 (NIV)

"To humans belong the plans of the heart, but from the Lord comes the proper answer of the tongue. All a person's ways seem pure to them, but motives are weighed by the Lord." – Proverbs 16:1-2 (NIV)

The matter of the heart is the heart of the matter. Purity in the heart is a qualification to see God and to hear Him clearly. The account of our heart is a critical matter that requires diligent work and careful attention. If your heart is not circumcised, it can deceive you. No wonder the scriptures says we must keep the heart with all diligence for out of it flows the issues of life (Proverbs 4:23).

TYPES OF HEART

A REPENTANT HEART

"Create in me a pure heart, O God, and renew a steadfast spirit within me. Do not cast me from your presence or that your Holy Spirit from me." – Psalm 51:10-11 (NIV)

A repentant heart is the type of heart that sees the awfulness of its many sins and iniquities for which Jesus has died on the cross. A repentant heart is moved with deep heartfelt Godly sorrow over its sinful ways.

"My sacrifice, O God, is a broken spirit; a broken and contrite heart you, God, will not despise." – Psalm 51:17 (NIV)

The blood of Jesus cleanses our hearts from all sins and unrighteousness. God is always pleased with a repentant heart. A repentant heart is a heart of humility. The Holy Spirit shines forth His light upon a repentant heart and dispels every darkness to make the heart viable for God to connect with.

A NEW HEART

This is the heart of a former sinner saved by God's grace and mercy. The new and purified heart is the temple of God, the home of God, the Father, the Son and Holy Spirit, according to the promise of the Lord Jesus Christ. "...Anyone who loves me will obey my teaching. My Father will love them, and we will come to them and make our home with them." – John 14:23 (NIV)

"Therefore, if anyone is in Christ, the new creation has come: the old has gone, the new is here!" – 2 Corinthians 5:17 (NIV)

A HEART OF WISDOM

As believers in Christ Jesus, we are to be aware that we have a purpose in living to fulfill the course of His will for our lifetimes. In living each day, we should be seeking only to do His will. We are to be aware of not wasting our time, but using wisdom in how we redeem the time and conduct our affairs because our time is not in our hands but in God's hand.

"Our days may come to seventy years, or eighty, if our strength endures; yet the best of them are but trouble and sorrow, for they quickly pass, and we fly away. If only we knew the power of Your anger! Your wrath is as great as the fear that is Your due. Teach us to number our days that we may gain a heart of wisdom." – Psalm 90:10-12 (NIV)

When you receive understanding from God on how to spend your days, you will know that you are not allowed to spend it on frivolous things. You have a very short time here on Earth, compared to where you are going after your departure – eternity. It is what you do here that will prepare you for that eternity. Most importantly, your attitude towards and relationship with Christ determine your eternity.

A PURE HEART

A pure heart is that type of heart with an unflinching consecration in thoughts, imaginations and spoken words. The focus of someone who has experienced the truth, speaks the truth, obeys and appropriates the truth.

The person with a pure heart will always speak the truth from the heart and will not have delight in things that will bring reproach to his neighbours. He always updates the condition of his heart and aligns it with the mind of Christ. The heart must always be purged by the blood of Jesus from all evil and everything that is not right before God. When your heart is not right before God, nothing you do can be right before God. You will not be able to make a right decision according to the will of God.

Whatever you do with a wrong heart is futile, without any eternal value and reward. Little wonder, when God deals with the heart of any man He plans to use as an instrument in His hand, as He dealt with the heart of Moses.

THE HEART OF INTEGRITY

What is integrity of heart?

- Wholeness of heart.
- Sincerity and trustworthiness.
- Quality of being honest and upright.

Having integrity of heart is doing what is right and trustworthy at all times. To bring transformation to any nation and people, the heart must be established in integrity. All matters of government rest on this principle – the constitution may be good and the system or structure of government excellent however, if the administrators are not grounded in integrity, the nations will fail. No matter how spiritual a person is, without integrity of heart, he will not lead transformation successfully (Nehemiah 5:14-19).

The foundation of the heart must be laid with integrity and largeness of heart, for the fulfilment of Kingdom destiny. Having integrity of heart involves humility, radical obedience and loyalty. Integrity of heart and skillfulness of hands are the major ingredients for national transformation.

Paul became all things to all men with integrity of heart. When a leader leads with an integrity of heart, he will be able to do the work of transformation that yields eternal reward.

David shepherded Israel with integrity of heart and by the skillfulness of his hands.

"He chose David His servant and took him from the sheep pens; from tending the sheep He brought him to be the shepherd of his people Jacob, of Israel his inheritance. And David shepherded them with integrity of heart; with skillful hands he led them." – Psalm 78:70-72 (NIV)

When integrity fails, everything fails. Integrity of heart is an incorruptible heart, wholeness of heart. The nation can only be built by integrity of heart and skillfulness of hands.

A LION'S HEART

A believer with a lion's heart lives a confident life with a clear conscience before God and before everyone.

"The wicked flee though no one pursues, but the righteous are as bold as a lion." – Proverbs 28:1 (NIV)

A lion is never intimidated by other animals, but has authority with boldness and confidence to exercise dominion over all other animals in the forest.

Someone with a Lion's heart will not habour secret sins, error or any form of unrighteousness that will subject his

Kingdom identity to crisis and that will make him to fall for less and eventually be destroyed.

"But who can discern their own errors? Forgive my hidden faults. Keep Your servant also from willful sins; may they not rule over me. Then I will be blameless, innocent and of great transgression." – Psalm 19:12-13 (NIV).

AN UNDERSTANDING HEART

God ponders the hearts of every man by Himself. Therefore, it is imperative to have an understanding heart that can discern between evil and good. An understanding heart is a heart that is full of knowledge and understanding. A heart that knows when to reject evil and do all that pleases the heart of God.

A heart with a lack of understanding destroys marriages. Largeness of heart with understanding enable marriages to fulfill their Kingdom purpose and enhance strong marriage relationships.

"Your servant is here among the people you have chosen, a great people, too numerous to count or number. So give Your servant a discerning heart to govern your people and to distinguish between right and wrong. For who is able to govern this great people of Yours?" – 1 Kings 3:8-9 (NIV)

- Leadership, governance and operating from the throne is a serious affair.

- You are responsible for the lives of other people.

- Your decisions will affect people even beyond the borders of your nation.

- Wisdom or lack of it will bring prosperity or ruin to the nation.

- A heart that can discern what is good from evil.

- Wisdom is the extraordinary principle and skill in management.

LARGENESS OF HEART

God gave Solomon wisdom and understanding exceeding much, and largeness of heart, even as the sand that is on the seashore (1 Kings 4:29)

Largeness of heart helps to solve many problems. A narrow or small heart manifests foolishness. Pride is a manifestation of foolishness. A product of narrow mindedness is when you fail to see the bigger picture of the problem. The root of incompetence comes from a narrow heart. Leaders need much wisdom and largeness of heart.

AN HONEST HEART

"You deserve honesty from the heart; yes, utter sincerity and truthfulness. Oh, give me this wisdom." – Psalm 51:6 (TLB)

Honesty in the heart:

- Truthfulness

- Genuineness

- Sincerity

Being honest with ourselves, others and God requires admitting we are imperfect. Doing so is humbling, but the rewards are worth it.
Honesty—admitting when we have messed up—opens the door for forgiveness, reconciliation, and restoration. It paves the way for us to grow in wisdom and learn from our mistakes.

AN OBEDIENT HEART

"But Samuel replied: Does the Lord delight in burnt offerings and sacrifices as much as in obeying the Lord? To obey is better than sacrifice and to hear is better than the fat of rams. For rebellion is like the sin of divination, and arrogance like the

evil of idolatry. Because you have rejected the word of the Lord, He has rejected you as King." – 1 Samuel 15:22-23 (NIV)

- Obedience is better than sacrifice.

- There is no partial obedience – God removed king Saul for disobedience.

- There is a need to deal with stubbornness.

- There is a need to deal with rebellion.

- There is a need to pray for a heart of obedience.

- The heart of compassion

A compassionate heart is the type of heart that is always willing to help others, a heart that carries others along. Being thoughtful of others sincerely from your heart to help others out of their pains.

When you set aside your indifference and connect with those who are in pain, and having a feeling of deep sympathy and sorrow for another who is stricken by misfortune, accompanied by a strong desire to alleviate the suffering. (Matthew 20:34)

Jesus moved with compassion:

"When Jesus landed and saw a large crowd, He had compassion on them, because they were like sheep without a shepherd. So He began teaching them many things." – Mark 6:34 (NIV)

You must allow the Holy Spirit to change your heart from a heart of indifference and cruelty to a heart of compassion.

A DETRIBALISED HEART

Tribalism is a terrible state of being organised in a tribe and having the behaviour and attitudes that stem from strong loyalty to one's own tribe or social group.

To be qualified to use the keys of the Kingdom, you have to detribalise your heart. No matter the level of your office or position in the Church, as believers in Jesus Christ, tribalism is a sin and God hates any form of sin and unrighteous attitude.

God is not white, black or coloured, He is a spirit and they that worship Him must worship Him in spirit and in truth. Inter-tribal issues are weapons of destruction that the devil use most often to destroy nations, communities and territories.

It is imperative to rise and face this brutal fact and deal with tribalism in all areas of our society as the Ecclesia with the keys of love and unity, so the gates of Hell will no longer prevail against the Church. Jesus has built His church upon the solid rock of His sovereign identity as the Son of the living God.

ENCUMBERED HEART

An encumbered heart is a type of heart that is impeded with the care for worldly things, which don't have eternal values. An encumbered heart will always stray away from God's presence and will not be able to hear the voice of the Lord, because of the burden that the heart is encumbered with.

"May the words of my heart and this meditation of my heart be pleasing in your sight, Lord, my Rock and Redeemer." – Psalm 19:14 (NIV)

An encumbered heart is always distracted and eventually loses its focus. Distractions and wrong priorities shut the gates of Heaven upon your heart.
Unnecessary anxieties and worries can encumber your heart and invade it with darkness. When your heart is invaded with darkness, you will hardly hear the voice of the Lord!

"As Jesus and his disciples were on their way, he came to a village where a woman named Martha opened her home to

Him. She had a sister called Mary, who sat at the Lord's feet listening to what He said. But Martha was distracted by all the preparations that had to be made. She came to Him and asked, 'Lord, don't You care that my sister has left me to do the work by myself? Tell her to help me!' 'Martha, Martha," the Lord answered, 'you are worried and upset about many things, but few things are needed – or indeed only one. Mary has chosen what is better, and it will not be taken away from her.'" – Luke 10:38-42 (NIV).

AN EVIL HEART

An evil heart is a disobedient heart. When you fail to obey the voice of God, He counts it as an evil heart. Partial obedience is disobedience.

"Why did you not obey the Lord? Why did you pounce on the plunder and do evil in the eyes of the Lord?" – 1 Samuel 15:19 (NIV)

Anyone who detests correction and rebels against God's voice is a rebellious person and is also an idol worshipper, which is wickedness against God. You worship your own will in your heart when you disobey the voice and the commandment of God. Disobedience to God's word is wickedness against God.

"But I gave them this command: Obey me, and I will be your God and you will be My people. Walk in obedience to all I

command you, that it may go well with you. But they did not listen or pay attention; instead, they followed the stubborn inclinations of their evil hearts. They went backwards and not forward." – Jeremiah 7:23-24 (NIV).

BACKSLIDDEN HEART

This is the hardened heart, a heart that has turned against God and rebels against God the Father. A backslidden heart is like a dog that goes back to its vomit and like a pig that has been washed but goes back to roll in the mud.

A backslidden heart has a dim conscience.

Although he might still be a churchgoer, hiding his worldliness under a cloak of religion, the love of God has grown cold in his heart. He is surrounded by temptations to which he has given in instead of resisting them. The cross of Jesus is no longer carried with joy and gladness, but becomes an unwelcome, heavy load.

"And, But My righteous one will live by faith. And I take no pleasure in the one who shrinks back. But we do not belong to those who shrink back and are destroyed, but to those who have faith and are saved." – Hebrews 10:38-39 (NIV).

A FOOLISH HEART

"The fool says in his heart, 'There is no God.' They are corrupt, and their ways are vile; there is no one who does good." – Psalm 15:1 (NIV)

A foolish person is someone who lacks good sense of judgement and acts unwisely. When you fail to seek the knowledge of the truth and have a clear understanding of who you are, your divine personality and the identity of your creator, you might be very unwise. A foolish person who lacks understanding of the truth of God's sovereignty will be easily deceived.

"The Lord looks down from heaven on all mankind to see if there are any who understand, any who seek God. All have turned away, all have become corrupt; there is no one who does good, not even one. Do all these evildoers know nothing? They devour My people as though eating bread; they never call on the Lord." – Psalm 14: 2 – 4 (NIV)

A foolish person will detest the knowledge of the will of God. Their heart will always stray away from the knowledge of the truth of the word of God. Their heart will always deceive them.

CIRCUMCISION OF THE HEART

Our works on Earth are measured by what goes on in our heart. Since God deals directly with our hearts, all our work will also be judged based on the state of our heart. Moses missed the promise land because of the state of his heart!

We will receive our eternal reward through the dealings in our heart. No wonder Paul prayed passionately for the eyes of his heart to be enlightened.

"I pray that they eyes of your heart may be enlightened in order that you may know the hope to which He has called you, the riches of His glorious inheritance in His holy people," – Ephesians 1:18 (NIV)

God will deal with issue of your heart before He uses you as a vessel of glory and honour in His hand. He also reveals His secrets to those who have a pure heart because the heart of man is God's candle and the heart of man is in the hand of God. It is therefore imperative to circumcise the heart daily and clean your heart from all evil imagination, evil thoughts and all unrighteousness for the heart to be able to connect with the Throne of God. Purity of heart is the only and one thing that qualifies you from seeing the Lord.

"Blessed are the pure in heart for they shall see God." Matthew 5:8 (NIV)

When your heart goes astray from God, He stops speaking to you. If you have been hearing God before distinctly and suddenly you do not hear God's voice anymore, check the state of your heart

PROBLEMS OF THE HEART

- **Unbelief** – Unbelief is an evil heart that is not stable. We see that some could never enter their rest as God's promised because of unbelief.

"See to it, brothers and sisters, that none of you has a sinful, unbelieving heart that turns away from the living God. But encourage one another daily, as long as it is called 'Today', so that none of you may be hardened by sin's deceitfulness." – Hebrews 3:12-13 (NIV)

This is very critical. When you doubt the word of God in your heart and refuse to believe His word and counsel, Satan uses it as a weapon to prevail over the inheritance of the saints.

"Let us, therefore, make every effort to enter that rest, so that no one will perish by following their example of disobedience. For the word of God is alive and active. Sharper than any double-edged sword, it penetrates even to dividing soul and spirit, joints and marrow; it judges the thoughts and attitudes of the heart." – Hebrews 4:11-12 (NIV)

God desires that we completely put our trust in Him without doubt in our heart.

"As has just been said: 'Today, if you hear His voice, do not harden your hearts as you did in the rebellion." - Hebrews 3:15 (NIV)

- *Wrong focus* – When you do not have God's perspectives in all things, you begin to lose your Kingdom focus and don't have your priorities right. Your heart can deceive you when you have a wrong focus.

"Let the words of my mouth and the meditation of my heart be acceptable in Your sight, O Lord, my strength and my Redeemer". Psalm 19:14

- *Fear of man and anxiety* – Fear is not part of the Kingdom benefits you have received from God. The fear of man is the beginning of bondage but the fear of God is the beginning of wisdom. Fear is a spirit of bondage, which God has not given to you, but originated from the devil with its torment.

"For God has not given us a spirit of fear, but of power and of love and of a sound mind." - 2 Timothy 1:7 (NKJV)

- *Frustration of the heart* – The heart can be frustrated when there is betrayal of trust. When you put your trust in man instead of God, your heart can be frustrated. Jesus did not commit Himself into the hand of any man. He knew no man in the flesh but in the spirit.

- *Rejection and self-pity* – Do not give power to anyone to break your heart. There is no one who has authority over your heart. Your heart is in the hand of God, so open the gate of your heart only to God to dwell in your heart. No man can frustrate you and break your heart except if you give the person access. Your happiness and joy is in God's hand and in your hand. The joy of the Lord is your strength.

"Scorn has broken my heart and has left me helpless; I looked for sympathy, but there was none, for comforters, but I found none." – Psalm 69:20 (NIV)

- *Stubbornness of heart* – God counts stubbornness in the heart as witchcraft, and the judgement on the spirit of witchcraft is death. A stubborn and unfaithful heart always strays from God.

"For rebellion is like the sin of divination, and arrogance like the evil of idolatry..." 1 Samuel 15:23 (NIV)

194

- **Root of bitterness** – When you fail to pursue peace with all men based on God's word, the devil will rob you of the grace of God and plant bitterness in your heart. When bitterness is planted in the heart, it forms a stronghold which makes you fall short of the grace of God. The root of bitterness in the heart of a man causes defilement (Hebrews 12:12-14).

- **Pride and arrogance** – Pride goes before destruction. God is very far to a proud person. Pride erodes grace from your life.

"But He gives us more grace. That is why the Scripture says: God opposes the proud but shows favour to the humble," – James 4:6 (NIV)

The election and calling of God is according to the issue of the heart. The Lord must purge the eyes of our hearts so that we can effectively use the keys of the Kingdom to rule and reign with the Kingdom principles and new order. As we change our hearts, He will change our guards.

According to God's Kingdom principles, He wants us to circumcise our hearts so we can see His glory, see as He sees, decree as he decrees and use our Kingdom authority to exercise judgment upon the kingdom of darkness and dominate our Kingdom inheritance to the glory of God's name.

Strategic prayers

- Lord, circumcise my heart afresh.

- I lay my heart upon the altar, at the Throne of grace; cleanse my heart from all impurities, O Lord.

- I plead the blood of Jesus upon the table of my heart.

- Lord, enlighten the eyes of my heart.

THE INTEGRITY PROMISE – Psalm 101 (KJV)

"I will sing of mercy and judgment: unto thee, O Lord, will I sing.

I will behave myself wisely in a perfect way. O when wilt thou come unto me? I will walk within my house with a perfect heart.

I will set no wicked thing before mine eyes: I hate the work of them that turn aside; it shall not cleave to me.

A froward heart shall depart from me: I will not know a wicked person.

Whoso privily slandereth his neighbour, him will I cut off: him that hath an high look and a proud heart will not I suffer.

Mine eyes shall be upon the faithful of the land that they may dwell with me: he that walketh in a perfect way, he shall serve me.

He that worketh deceit shall not dwell within my house: he that telleth lies shall not tarry in my sight.

I will early destroy all the wicked of the land; that I may cut off all wicked doers from the city of the Lord."

Song for a clean heart – Psalm 51: 10-12 (KJV)

"Create in me a clean heart, O God; and renew a right spirit within me.

Cast me not away from thy presence; and take not thy holy spirit from me."

Restore unto me the joy of thy salvation; and uphold me with thy free spirit."

CHAPTER 12

THE KEY OF GOD'S GRACE

"We have different gifts, according to the grace given to each of us. If your gifts is prophesying, then prophesy in accordance with your faith; if it is serving, then serve; if it is teaching, then teach; if it is to encourage, then give encouragements; if it is giving, then give generously; if it is to lead, do it diligently; if it is to show mercy, do it cheerfully." – Romans 12:6-8 (NIV)

"For it is by grace you have been saved, through faith – and this is not form yourselves, it is the gift of God – not by works, so that no one can boast." – Ephesians 2:8-9 (NIV)

Grace is God's unmerited favour for us. Grace is an immense strength and we receive daily Kingdom benefits from the Lord as believers in Christ Jesus. Grace is God's kindness towards us who believe.

To Esther, grace was unmerited favour and uncommon strength (Esther 5:1-8).

To Ruth, grace was an uncommon strength and divine ability (Ruth 1-3)

Grace enables believers to live above sins. The understanding of the deep meaning of the grace of our Lord Jesus Christ will enhance our ability to appropriate the power to prevail over sins and be filled with the supernatural power and the anointing of the gifts of God. There is a covenant of grace and we need to draw from the Throne of Grace that Jesus Christ has earned for us through the sacrifice of His blood.

UNDERSTANDING THE POWER OF GRACE

"By the grace of God, I am what I am, and his grace toward me was not in vain. On the contrary, I worked harder than any of them, though it was not I, but the grace of God that is with me". *(1 Corinthians 15:10)*

Grace is not simply leniency when we have sinned. John Piper remarked further in his Solid Joy daily devotional, that grace is the enabling gift and power of God not to sin. Grace is power, not just pardon.

This is plain, for example, in 1 Corinthians 15:10. Paul describes grace as the enabling power of his work. It is not simply the pardon of his sins; it is the power to press on in obedience. "I worked harder than any of them, though it was not I, but the grace of God that is with me."

Therefore, the effort we make to obey God is not an effort done in our own strength, but "by the strength that God supplies — in order that in everything God may be glorified" (1 Peter 4:11). It is the obedience of faith. Faith in God's ever-arriving gracious power to enable us to do what we should.

Paul confirms this in 2 Thessalonians 1:11–12 by calling each of our acts of goodness a "work of faith," and by saying that the glory this brings to Jesus is "according to the grace of our God" because it happens "by his power." Listen for all those phrases:

To this end we always pray for you, that our God may make you worthy of his calling and may fulfill every resolve for good and every work of faith by his power, so that the name of our Lord Jesus may be glorified in you, and you in him, according to the grace of our God and the Lord Jesus Christ.

The obedience that gives God pleasure is produced by the power of God's grace through faith. The same dynamic is at work at every stage of the Christian life. The power of God's grace that saves through faith (Ephesians 2:8) is the same power of God's grace that sanctifies through faith.

Jesus Christ, in obedience to the will of the Father, He died a shameful death and ascended up on high to present the blood and sit at the right hand of God. He is watching, advocating and waiting until our adversary, the devil becomes our footstool.

Jesus has finished His own assignment on Earth. It is now our responsibility to draw from the victory and the intercession He is making on our behalf in the inner court of Heaven with legal evidence of His blood. He has finished the work and earned the everlasting victory for us. We only need to key into the victory on the legal ground that He paid in full with the sacrifice of His blood and the pain He bore on our behalf.

The different gifts He gave unto every man and the grace to operate the gifts was earned by the transaction and the battle that He fought inside the grave by the help of the Holy Spirit, which was the grace Jesus Himself had while He was living in the flesh. Jesus had to live in the flesh and humble Himself for Him to be able to shed His blood as a sacrifice for us.

Although He was God, He had to live in the flesh to shed the blood of the new covenant because spirit cannot die and shed His blood. The good news therefore is that to every believer there are spiritual gifts that have been released unto us with a measure of grace to operate these spiritual gifts.

Jesus had to destroy the power of death and darkness inside the grave where He led captivity captive and destroyed the veil and cover over our potential. He broke the wall of partition that limited our potential, restricted our gifts, and kept us in the box of ignorance.

He led captivity captive and collected the keys from Satan. He opened the door for an easy access to the holiest of all through His blood for us to go beyond the veil and manifest the glory and power of God. He released grace upon us according to the measure of the gifts He has given unto us in His own likeness to fill all things and fulfil our Kingdom destinies.

"And I tell you that you are Peter, and on this rock I will build My church, and the gates of Hades will not overcome it, I will give you the keys of the kingdom of heaven; whatever you bind on earth will be bound in heaven, and whatever you loose on earth will be loosed in heaven." – Matthew16:18-19 (NIV)

Jesus Christ earned the Kingdom authority that was stolen through disobedience and rebellion back unto us. He led captivity captive and released us from the captivity we have put ourselves in through sins and iniquities. The implication of this is that after we are born again we have easy access to the keys of the Kingdom and the delegated authority to reign, rule, subdue and dominate our Kingdom inheritance.

There is no more limitation, ignorance, stagnancy, defeat and death.

Sins and iniquities rob us of our authority and deny the power thereof. When we practice unrighteousness, we lose our authority and the power to reign, rule, subdue and dominate. We suffer defeat instantly. The devil often looks forward to this opportunity to wreak havoc on believers' kingdom inheritance.

The battle that the devil is fighting daily by roaming about like a roaring lion is to destroy believers and steal their Kingdom inheritance. The battle the devil is fighting from the Garden of Eden is the battle of our Kingdom inheritance

THE RELEASED GRACE

"As each one has received a gift, minister it to one another, as good stewards of the manifold grace of God".

Peter the apostle emphasised the varied grace of God in his exhortation here. Grace was earned by the blood sacrifice of Jesus and given unto everyone without exception to appropriate the grace to fulfil God's eternal kingdom purpose through Jesus Christ.

We are not supposed to misuse the grace of God and neither receive the grace in vain or take it for granted. When you live in sin and iniquity, you decrease the grace of God upon your life.

Although, the gifts of God are without repentance, but sins drain away the power and the anointing upon the gifts of God, which is the grace, which supposed to show forth the glory of God. God gives grace to the humble and those who obey His commandments, but the proud He knows a far off.

Samson took the grace of God for granted with his perpetual sins with Delilah, he died with the Philistines.

"And she said, "The Philistines are upon you, Samson!" So he awoke from his sleep, and said, "I will go out as before, at other times, and shake myself free!" But he did not know that the Lord had departed from him." Then the Philistines took him and put out his eyes, and brought him down to Gaza. They bound him with bronze fetters, and he became a grinder in the prison."

The grace of God was earned by the blood of Jesus and given unto us in measured sizes according to the spiritual gifts given to each one to operate the spiritual gifts God has given unto us.

The grace of God is being released according to the need in the body of Christ. The purpose of your spiritual gifts are for the edification of the body of Christ, they are not for you and your household. They are meant to edify the body of Christ and perfect the redemptive, the work of Calvary.

Grace and strength is released daily to appropriate your spiritual gifts for the equipping of the saints for the work of ministry, for the edifying of the body of Christ, till we all come to the unity of the faith and of the knowledge of the son of God, to a perfect man, to the measure of the stature of the fullness of Christ.

All believers in Jesus Christ are qualified to withdraw grace from the throne of God according to the measure of the gift of God that is given to you to manifest His glory.

As you withdraw money from the Automated Teller Machine (ATM) anytime you have a need of money, you can likewise approach the Throne of God to withdraw the measure of grace needed to utilise your gifts and potential that God has given to you.

OPERATIONAL PRINCIPLES TO USE THE KEY OF GRACE

- Acknowledge the price Jesus has paid with His blood and the pain He bore on your behalf.

- Appreciate and give thanks for the spiritual gifts He has earned and given to you for the edification of His body and fulfilment of His Kingdom purposes.

- Appreciate and give thanks to the Lord for the measure of the grace He has earned and given to you through His blood to operate your spiritual gifts and fulfil your Kingdom purpose on Earth.

- Repent for lack of knowledge and understanding of the power of the grace. Repent for misusing and taking the grace of God for granted over the years.

- Destroy every covering of darkness over your spiritual gifts, potential and your life (Isaiah 25:7-8).

- Command the light of God to shine upon your gifts and potential to begin to manifest the power and glory of God.

- Draw and secure an unprecedented grace through the covenant of grace made with us by the blood of the everlasting covenant from the Throne of grace daily upon your gifts to begin to run distances without measure to fulfil your kingdom destinies.

- Appropriate grace to re-possess all your Kingdom inheritance and your delegated Kingdom authority.

CHAPTER 13

JESUS USED THE SEVEN KINGDOM KEYS

ADAM AND EVE LOST THE KINGDOM KEYS.

Adam and Eve were created and kept in the Garden of Eden with the keys to operate in the Kingdom and dominate all other things that God has created in the garden. Adam was given the key of the spoken word with divine authority to name all the animals. God created man in His own image with dignity, power and authority as His representatives on earth, to carry His glory and dominate the earth! Adam and Eve lost the keys due to their disobedience.

Every kingdom has keys that are used to operate the throne in the kingdom, as king and priest with the operational principles. God gave Adam the keys with legal authority to operate on the throne at Eden, to dominate the earth. He also gave them the operational principles to use the keys in the Garden. Satan, in his subtlety manipulated the operational principles of the keys because of the failure of Eve to use the key of a pure heart to guard the gate of her heart.

Satan understands dominion, this is why he roams about like a roaring lion every day, looking for opportunities to deceive the people of God and steal their Kingdom dominion and the inheritance of the Saints of God! Satan stole Adam and Eve's inheritance and the keys to their dominion.

Legal authority was given to human beings to have dominion on Earth. Dominion is the matter of the Kingdom you dominate and rule in a domain as king and priest. You exercise your authority in a domain where you have influence.

After Satan stole the keys from Adam and Eve, God in His infinite mercy and compassion came to the earth in a physical body for Him to be a legal entity on Earth. He used Mary and came to the earth as God in a man's body to retrieve the KINGDOM KEYS and to restore the dominion and the glory.

The child was the body that carried the Son of God as a man on Earth. The Son used the child's legal body that developed in a woman's womb, was born, lived on Earth without sin and bore our sins, the pain, shed His blood and descended to Hell. , He conquered the grave to collect the keys of the Kingdom from Satan and return the keys to the Saints to reign, rule, subdue kingdoms of darkness and dominate the earth for His glory.

HOW JESUS USED THE KEYS OF THE KINGDOM

"And I tell you that you are Peter, and on this rock I will build My church, and the gates of Hades will not overcome it, I will give you the keys of the kingdom of heaven; whatever you bind on earth will be bound in heaven, and whatever you loose on earth will be loosed in heaven." – Matthew16:18-19 (NIV)

Whatever you allow on Earth with your legal authority will be allowed in Heaven. God gave human beings legal authority to govern the earth. This is why God will not act and interfere on the affairs of man on Earth until man gives God permission to act through prayers and intercessions. Nothing happens on Earth without the legal permission by the priests and kings that are ruling and reigning on Earth.

A gate as an entity will not move without using the right keys and the right operational principles and strategies. The gates represent a major determinant in taking possession of your Kingdom inheritance.

Jesus Himself dealt with the gates before He could access the keys. Jesus spoke to the gates to be lifted with authority! He used the key of the spoken word!

"Lift up your heads, O ye gates! And be lifted up, ye everlasting doors! And the King of glory shall come in. Who is this King of

glory? The Lord strong and mighty, The Lord mighty in battle. Lift up your heads, O ye gates! Lift up, ye everlasting doors! And the King of glory shall come in. Who is this King of glory? The Lord of hosts, He is the King of glory." – Psalm 24:7-10 (KJV)

Gates can hear the spoken word. Gates are access to possession, authority and power. Keys release the generational blessings and give access to your inheritance.

KEYS OF REPENTANCE AND FORGIVENESS

Jesus used the keys of repentance and forgiveness on the cross of Calvary. The thief that repented on the cross received immediate forgiveness and made heaven at the last minute.

KEY OF THE BLOOD OF JESUS

Jesus presented His blood at the grave as an evidence to possess the gates of Hell. He challenged the devil that has the power over death with the blood of the righteous that he shed on the cross. He broke the power of the grave and led captivity captives by the power of the blood of the everlasting covenant.

THE KEYS OF UNITY AND LOVE

Jesus Christ always worked in unison with the Father, He never did anything alone. He was always in agreement with the heavenly Father because they are one. He always gave thanks to God in Heaven upon the food He gives to thousands of people. He declared: "I and My Father are one."

"I and My Father are one." John 10:30

THE KEY OF THE HOLY SPIRIT

Jesus went about doing good by the power of the Holy Spirit. He overthrew the cohorts of the devil by the power of the Holy Spirit. Jesus Christ prevailed and was qualified to take the scroll from the Father that sat upon the Throne through the seven Spirits of God and seven horns anointing which is the fullness of the Holy Spirit.

THE KEYS OF THE WORD AND VOICE OF GOD

Jesus Christ used the key of the word to raise the dead, heal the sick and deliver the oppressed. He used the spoken word to rebuke the devil at every point of temptation. His words are very powerful. At the tomb of Lazarus, He called Lazarus forth with the spoken word and Lazarus came out of the grave!

"Then they took away the stone from the place where the dead man was lying. And Jesus lifted up His eyes and said, Father, I thank you that You have heard Me. And I know that You always hear Me, but because of the people who are standing by I said this, that they may believe that You sent Me. Now when He had said these things, He cried with a loud voice, Lazarus, come forth!
And he who had died came out bound hand and foot with grave clothes, and his face was wrapped with a cloth. Jesus said to them, loose him, and let him go." John 11:41-44

Jesus Himself was the word. He used the spoken word to dispel darkness.

He used the key of the word, to create reform and restore. Jesus taught the disciples through the spoken word.

THE KEY OF GRACE

Jesus Christ Himself is the God of grace. He drew grace at the point of every need from the throne of grace because He was in a body and living on the earth. He drew grace more abundantly at Gethsemane when He was negotiating with the Father, if the cup could be taken away from Him before crucifixion!

Jesus drew grace from the Father in heaven at the point of distress, but the disciples were unable to use the key of grace. Little wonder they fell into temptation as Peter cut off one of the ears of the accuser who came to arrest Jesus.

When you enter into a point of distress, there is an opportunity given to you as believer in Christ Jesus to draw grace from the throne of grace and be strengthened to fulfill your Kingdom mandate without failing.

THE KEY OF A PURE HEART

Jesus' heart is full of compassion and absolute purity. Without a pure heart, no man shall see God. Jesus used the key of a pure heart to relate with the Father and with His disciples and even the Pharisees. Whenever the Pharisees came to tempt Jesus with hard questions, He could discern their hearts because he was God the Son.

CHAPTER 14

FAITH – THE MASTER KEY

FAITH TO USE THE SEVEN KINGDOM KEYS

Faith is believing what you have not seen as it is existing, having absolute trust in God and holding tight on to God without wavering or doubting. Doubt is the enemy of faith.

While faith sees the way, doubt sees the wilderness. While faith sees the emergence of a new day, doubt sees the darkest night. Doubt fears to take a step and faith soars to the altitude like an eagle. Doubt often questions why.

Faith declares that I believe Lord and ask Him to banish my unbelief. Faith remains undaunted and unflinching. Faith sets its face like a flint while doubt fills its face with despair and agitations.

A strong conviction in the act of God's providence will make you stand strong in the face of adversity, challenges and problems. When you are sure of the One you believe in and worship with fear, love and reference with all your heart, you can face anything.

It is crucial to have faith before we can effectively use the seven keys of the Kingdom to rule, reign, subdue kingdoms and dominate the earth to the glory of God.

TYPES OF FAITH

FAITH THAT SEES

The faith that sees is a type of faith that acts based on the revelation of God's word through open and night vision. When a revelation is received from God and is observed by faith and seen in vision, if it is believed and called forth into reality—the invisible becomes visible.

By faith, we call forth the things that are not as though they are. Faith sees with spiritual eyes and nurtures the vision with God-given imagination. The vision takes hold of the person and because of faith. They will not let go until it has come forth.

The vision is conceived on the inside by observing it in spirit and it becomes established by declaration of faith in words. Faith Marie Baczko said that our internal capacity to conceive must increase and the wineskin of the mind refashioned to contain the largeness of God's revelation. We hold on to it by faith and occupy the revelation by giving it a place of prominence in our hearts.

The battle to give birth is a decision to fight for what we believe. Begin to SEE the door opening to your opportunity, visualize it, embrace it and declare it!

"And by faith even Sarah, who was past childbearing age, was enabled to bear children because she considered Him faithful who had made the promise." – Hebrews 11:11 (NIV)

Firstly, the miracle came forth by faith because Sarah believed. Secondly, she counted Him faithful who had made the promise. Sarah had experienced the faithfulness of God in her life on many occasions. The word for faith used in this scripture is pistis, which in Greek means "good faith, trust and reliability", which is conviction of the truthfulness of God. Sarah received strength to conceive. The Greek word for strength is Dunamis, which means miraculous, supernatural power.

Sarah's mind was renewed by faith in God. She saw, she believed, she trusted, thereby establishing a foundation of faith for all future generations. Sarah decided, she made the decision to act on the promise that marked out the course of her life. She occupied the revelation, believed it, nurtured it, and brought forth a child in old age. Sarah's faith released the explosive, miraculous, Dunamis power of God to break forth in her body and in her life.

You have to occupy the revelations God has given you and hold on to them. Begin to see and observe God's vision for your life. Decide in agreement with God, and then frame the future within those parameters with His Word. God has given us partnership and Sonship with divine authority and power to use the seven keys of the Kingdom to overcome all circumstances in all sphere of life!

DOUBTLESS FAITH

Our heavenly Father has no favorites in His kingdom. He does not value one over another. His love and provision is accessible by everyone He has created according to the measure of faith that each one possesses. All that He has made already exists and can be accessed through faith in Him. Make your way through doubt and unbelief, sweep away the cobwebs of confusion and ask in faith.

"Have faith in God," Jesus answered. "Truly I tell you, if anyone says to this mountain, 'Go, throw yourself into the sea,' and does not doubt in their heart but believes that what they say will happen, it will be done for them." – Mark 11:22-23 (NIV)

This scripture comes from an incident when Jesus spoke to a fig tree and it dried up because it did not have fruit to feed Him when He was hungry.

Since the fig tree failed to fulfill its purpose, to bear fruit in its season to feed the hungry, Jesus spoke a word and it took hold on the fig tree immediately. Jesus then told His disciples to have the faith of God! In other words, Jesus was implying that the disciples could have and use the same faith that God uses. We need to have the same faith that God uses to change His environment, circumstances and situations.

FAITH THAT SPEAKS

The faith of God always speaks. God's faith is applied through speaking. Jesus says that whosoever says to this mountain to be removed without doubt it shall be so. Jesus was saying that we need to speak to our mountains, whether it is sickness, debt, failed marriage, relationship, unemployment, or lack.

What do we say to the mountains? We can command them to be moved from our lives and sight and be cast into the sea. Many of us, when we are facing mountains, we pray to God and ask Him to move the mountains on our behalf. But this is not what He said. Jesus did not say that we must ask God to move the mountain but we need to speak to the mountains like He spoke to the fig tree and the mountains will obey us.

It is through speaking that we create our world and apply our God given authority. Have you ever heard a saying that we are the product of our environment and our surroundings? Satan would like us to believe this statement so we feel like victims and therefore can do nothing to change our environment and circumstances. This statement is only true if we allow the environment and circumstances to shape our words, action and life.

We can choose to stop the environment and circumstances from shaping our lives by deciding to speak words of faith from our hearts over our environment and circumstances without doubt in our hearts. Strictly speaking, we are products of our own words and not our environment or circumstances. If we speak negative words over our lives and families, we get negative results and the reverse is true.

Some years ago, I was ministering in Chennai, India. I had preached in three churches on this Sunday. When you preach in a church in India, you must be prepared to minister to each individual in the congregation. I was exhausted after we had finished at the last church. We were driven on a tricycle and on our way, a cream-colored big snake that l have not seen in my life before was lying on our way.

The driver just exclaimed and stopped. Because l was exhausted, I just rebuked the snake and passed a death sentence to it without doubt in my heart. Amazingly, this snake died instantly! All the four people inside the tricycle

were amazed and started to tell me that I would be able to kill
a human being with the word of my mouth because in India they actually worship a snake goddess!

In order to effectively use the seven keys of the Kingdom to prevail over the gates of Hell, to rule, reign, subdue the kingdom of darkness, and dominate our Kingdom inheritance, we need unflinching faith without doubt in our hearts.

Jesus Christ never doubted the Father in heaven at every point when He needed to perform miracles because He knew He has given Him the authority and power to execute His counsel here on Earth.

God does not respond to grumbling, desperation and complaining but will always respond to faith based on His word. The Lord Jesus died to give us the full right of appropriating all the promises contained in His word. A lack or deficiency in any area of our lives is not due to what He has not done, but it is often due to what we are not doing right to appropriate these promises in our lives.

"Say to them, 'As I live,' says the LORD, 'just as you have spoken in My hearing, so I will do to you:" – Numbers 14:28 (NKJV)

I continuously speak the words of faith over my life, my family, my work situation and every area of my life. These words happen in my life. I therefore live an abundant life that is beyond limitations. I am not subject of environment and circumstance but they (environment and circumstances) are subjects of my authority in Christ!

Our soul is comprised of mind, will and emotion and is easily impacted by the trials and circumstances of life if not fiercely guarded and protected by faith in Christ—the Divine Shield that protects from all the elements of life.

If the mind is not guarded it will easily be infiltrated by fear, doubt and unbelief. These are the fruit of an orphan identity and identity theft. The devil always seeks an opportunity to steal our inheritance by exchanging our faith with fear, worries, anxiety and torment!

God has not given to us the spirit of fear in all what He has given to us, fear is excluded! As His Kingdom Citizen who supposed to manage His kingdom resources and dominate the earth for His glory.

STRATEGIC OPERATIONAL PRINCIPLES

In order to effectively use the seven keys of the Kingdom, you must receive what God promised in His word, and do these four things accordingly:

1. First, make up your mind. Take hold of His promise and do not let go. Be tenacious! God responds to a faith that perseveres and a mind that is made up: *"With God all things are possible." (Matthew 19:26)*

2. Second, visualise your victory. By faith, Abraham "saw" his children; he counted them every time he looked up at the stars (Genesis 15:5). That is what David did when he slew Goliath. Look your giant squarely in the face and declare, "You're coming down in the name of the Lord."

3. Third, speak to your situation. Jesus said: *"Whoever says to this mountain..." (Mark 11:23)* In this scripture Jesus used the word "believe" once, but referred to what you "say'" three times. Speak the word of God to your problem! Refuse to just talk and complain about your problem! Line up what you say with God's Word. Make His Word your word, and the mountain will become your servant!

4. Fourth, deal with the spirit of fear. If you let fear control your life, it will keep you from reaching your destiny. What a price! Fear breeds inaction, inaction

breeds lack of knowledge, lack of knowledge breeds ignorance, and ignorance breeds fear. If you are caught in this cycle, then here are some 'fear fighters' to help you to use the seven keys of the kingdom and prevail.

"Peace I leave with you; My peace I give you. I do not give to you as the world gives. Do not let your hearts be troubled and do not be afraid." – John 14:27 (NIV)

All these promises are for all the citizens of God's Kingdom to rule and reign as kings and priests on the earth. As you use the seven keys of the Kingdom diligently with faith and boldness, you will no longer lose any battle on the earth and you will be among the OVERCOMERS!

CHAPTER 15

PROPHETIC DECLARATION

"But you are a chosen generation, a royal priesthood, a holy nation, His own special people, that you may proclaim the praises of Him who called you out of darkness into His marvelous light; who once were not a people but are now the people of God, who had not obtained mercy but now have obtained mercy." 1 Peter 2:9-10 (NKJV)

1. I am part of a chosen generation and a royal priesthood, a peculiar person, a royal king and priest, called to proclaim the praises of God my heavenly Father.

2. I proclaim my acceptable year is here, the time to favour me.

3. I proclaim my acceptable year to bring me to a rich fulfilment of my Kingdom destiny and God's purpose for my life on Earth.

4. I receive the outpouring of the water of the word of God to water every dry place in my life, calling and election.

5. I receive manifold throne grace in this my acceptable year of the Lord, to diligently seek the Lord, until He rains righteousness on me and restores my fortunes.

6. I will arise and shine for my light has come and the GLORY of the Lord is risen upon me.

7. The Lord will arise over me and His glory will be seen upon me.

8. Gentiles shall come to my light, and kings to the brightness of my rising, for it is my acceptable season.

9. My heart shall continually swell with JOY in this, my acceptable season, because the abundance of the sea shall be turned to me.

10. In this acceptable year of mine, the wealth of the gentiles shall come to me, the multitude of camels shall cover my land, the treasure of darkness and the hidden riches of secret places shall be given unto me for the fulfilment of my Kingdom mandate to the glory of God's name.

11. My gates shall be open continually; they shall not be shut day or night that men may bring to me the wealth of the gentiles and their kings in procession.

12. The Sun shall no longer be my light by day, nor for brightness shall the moon give light to me, but the Lord will be to me an everlasting light, and my God will be my GLORY!

13. My sun shall no longer go down, nor my moon withdraws itself; for the Lord will be my everlasting light!

14. The days of my mourning are ended; for the JOY of the Lord shall continually be my strength!

15. All my people shall be righteousness; they shall inherit the land and the kingdom forever and ever, that the name of God will be glorified! Amen

OTHER BOOKS BY THE AUTHOR

1. The power of Kingdom Identity

2. The 7 Spirits of God to unlock Kingdom Destiny

3. The Power of Covenantal Altar

4. The Mystery of God's Grace

5. Developing Learning skills

www.ingramcontent.com/pod-product-compliance
Lightning Source LLC
Chambersburg PA
CBHW070557100426
42744CB00006B/309